THE
SMALL
GROUP

Consulting Editor: Charles H. Page
Professor Emeritus   University of Massachusetts

THE SMALL GROUP

second edition

Michael S. Olmsted &
A. Paul Hare

RANDOM HOUSE 🏠 **NEW YORK**

Second Edition
987654321
Copyright © 1959, 1978 by Random House, Inc.

Library of Congress Cataloging in Publication Data

Olmsted, Michael S
The small group.
Bibliography: p.
Includes indexes.
1. Small groups.   I. Hare, Alexander Paul,
        1923-   joint author.   II. Title.
HM133.04   1978   301.18'5   77-16080
                    ISBN 0-394-32123-5

Manufactured in the United States of America

To Charles H. Page

To Patricia, Jeffrey, and Michael C. Olmsted

FOREWORD

Many of us concerned with the field of small-group research and its practical implications for our life today will be pleased to see this revision of Michael Olmsted's book, judiciously amplified and brought up to date by A. Paul Hare. Olmsted's book has several virtues that are still unrivaled, in my opinion. First, it is a manageably small book on an area that has become quite large by now, an area in which it has become increasingly difficult to see the forest for the trees, with dense thickets of facts that may entangle the optimistic explorer. It is important that explorers should not be discouraged, for they are the heirs to the field.

A second virtue of Olmsted's book is that it places the small group effectively in relation to both sociology and psychology, and in relation to the study of culture. Researchers as well as explorers tend to get trapped in local thickets, and even to settle down happily in places with a very limited view. Olmsted's book maintains a bird's-eye view.

A third virtue of the book is that it maintains a highly useful historical dimension. The reader gains a clear sense of early theories and studies, and of the way in which our knowledge of small groups has grown. A. Paul Hare, probably the prime historian of the field and author of its most recent encyclopedic handbook, has added some of the more important studies of recent date. The book stands again as one of the very best introductions to the field, still small enough to be carried in the pocket.

Robert F. Bales
May 11, 1977

PREFACE

Following its publication in 1959, *The Small Group* became the most widely used short introduction to the study of interpersonal relations in small groups. In preparing this second edition of the text I have followed the advice of Bernhardt Lieberman, who was asked by the publisher to comment on the possibilities for revision, by not attempting to "improve" the text nor to change the approach in any major way. Instead, most of the first edition has been retained as it was originally written. On occasion a reference to the author in the singular has been changed to plural, "sexist" terminology has been altered in many places to conform to current values, and some references to the literature have been updated where a more recent version of the same work is available.

Readers familiar with the first edition will find that Chapters 1 and 2 are essentially the same. Chapter 3 has been supplemented by a new case study. The remaining chapters have been updated at various points to include summaries of research on topics not represented in the literature at the time of publication of the first edition—such subjects, for example, as nonverbal behavior, personal space, and decision rules.

PREFACE

The reader will note that the text has an element of "sexist" bias, because most of the early research was done with male subjects. This happened in part because male groups, such as gangs, presented problems that required study; in part because most researchers were male; and in part because after World War II, in many cases the research funds came from the military, who were interested in military leadership.

Actually, most of the research results refer to the behavior of both men and women, but the general terminology does not reveal this clearly. In particular the quotations from authors writing in an earlier period are given without changes in text, so that the custom of referring to the generalized individual as "he" obscures cases where females were actually used. In the summaries of the more recent literature, for example, on the "risky shift" or nonverbal behavior, differences between males and females in their patterns of interaction are noted when they are cited in the literature.

The primary aim of this book is still to provide an introduction to the study of the small group. For the reader who wishes to go beyond the introductory stage, a short list of books and articles providing a record of the history of small-group research and a review of current research and theory is given at the end of the book.

Michael S. Olmsted died in 1960, only a year after publication of the first edition of *The Small Group*. In this second edition, it has been my aim to leave unchanged its long-proven excellence.

—A. Paul Hare
Beacon, New York
June 1977

CONTENTS

THE
SMALL
GROUP

chapter one
INTRODUCTION

"Reason is not come to repeat the universe but to fulfill it."

—SANTAYANA

This study has two aims—first, to serve as an introduction to an area of interest in sociology and psychology, and second, to organize and interpret a body of ideas and research. Correspondingly, it hopes to be useful to two groups of readers: those who are beginning to learn about the various subfields within sociology and psychology and those who are already immersed in the study of small groups.

The attempt to meet two purposes and two audiences, while presenting difficulties, is not without its pleasures and advantages. Newcomers and old-timers will, naturally enough, be interested in somewhat different problems and levels of argument: what intrigues one is likely to strike the other as unprofitable. On the other hand, the situation presents a challenge, and we have found that the twin purposes complement and support one another. The attempt to deal simply with fundamental issues has led to constructive rethinking of old problems; the reevaluation of professionally familiar complexities has made it seem possible to organize the field around a few basic notions. Any field, one may suppose, can gain something from attempts at reorganization, even if only the reassurance that the old ways are best. The study of small groups differs from many other fields in sociology and psychology in that there are few recognized "old ways." There has been much interest in small groups on the part of academics, social workers, people in business, and others, but little agreement as to just how the phenomenon is best approached. The spate of small-group research which has occurred in the last three decades has introduced new data and new systems of analysis, but to the unaided eye at least, the impression is still of a bazaar rather than of orderly progress. Thus everyone seems to have a different reason for pursuing the subject as well as a different plan for dealing with it once it is caught.

In sum, the study of small groups seemed to us to stand in considerable need of organization and interpretation. And so, this little book.

Lastly, largely for the benefit of professional colleagues, it may be useful to say what this study is not. Though it will be heavily involved with experimental findings, it is not an attempt to codify research results in terms of a minimum number of hypotheses (in the manner of Klein or Riecken and Homans).[1] Nor is it a history of social scientists' interest in the study of small groups (as undertaken by Faris, Wilson, or Shils).[2] This study draws upon such sources but aims to be something more elementary and at the same time more extensive. It is a survey—and, we fear, sometimes a rather critical one—of propositions and findings in the study of small (and of primary) groups, focusing on major approaches, assumptions, and problems, and organized in terms of a conception of social science deriving ultimately from the work of Talcott Parsons and Robert F. Bales. It holds as a basic postulate that small-group analysis is neither a separate discipline standing alongside sociology and psychology nor the basic framework for those disciplines. Its motto is, rather, that the sociology of small groups is only a special case of the sociology of all groups.

With this apparent truism—which is by no means universally accepted, even in theory—we may turn to our subject matter.

chapter two

THE STUDY OF GROUPS

TWO TRADITIONS

The contemporary situation in the study of groups may be clarified by recognizing two major lines of development. These may be designated the "external" or sociological and the "internal" or psychological traditions.

External

The external approach is basically that of the older sociological and historical schools of thought. Groups are conceived of as worth studying because they are the building blocks, so to speak, of the larger society that is the chief object of analysis. The group is viewed from outside, externally, as a cell in the social organism. The major concern is not with the internal operations of these cells but with their basic characteristics and functions in larger social entities. Insofar as representatives of this older tradition are concerned with groups (and not all of them are), they may be described as seeing *societies as groups* (in contrast to the newer, psychological tradition, which sees *groups as societies*).

This societies-as-groups approach has long held a recognized place in sociology. It has been standard operating procedure for authors of texts and other general works on sociological subjects to set forth typologies of groups: the voluntary and nonvoluntary group, the interest group, the territorial group, and so on.[1] While the systems of classification do not always agree in detail, the authors never question that groups play a significant part in human affairs.

In this societies-as-groups tradition there is generally little direct concern with experimental techniques designed to get at internal organization. There is, however, a central and explicit awareness of certain qualities of the relationships among group members. This awareness is reflected in the well-known dichotomy of "primary" and "secondary" groups.

The Primary Group.   In the primary group, members have warm, intimate, and "personal" ties with one another; their solidarity is unselfconscious, a matter of sentiment rather than calculation. Such groups are usually of the small, face-to-face sort, spontaneous in their interpersonal behavior and devoted, though not necessarily explicitly, to mutual or common ends. The friendship group, the gang, and especially the family are usually cited as the foremost examples of primary groups.

The concept of the primary group received its classic formulation at the hands of the American sociologist Charles H. Cooley. In some often-quoted passages of his book *Social Organization*, he writes as follows:

> By primary groups I mean those characterized by intimate face-to-face association and cooperation. They are primary in several senses, but chiefly in that they are fundamental in forming the social nature and ideals of the individual. The result of intimate association, psychologically, is a certain fusion of individualities in a common whole, so that one's self, for many purposes at least, is the common life and purpose of the group. Perhaps the simplest way of describing this wholeness is by saying that it is a "we"; it involves the sort of sympathy and mutual identification for which "we" is the natural expression. One lives in the feeling of the whole and finds the chief aims of his will in that feeling.

7

It is not to be supposed that the unity of the primary group is one of mere harmony and love. It is always a differentiated and usually a competitive unity, admitting of self-assertion and various appropriative passions; but these passions are socialized by sympathy, and come, or tend to come, under the discipline of a common spirit. The individual will be ambitious, but the chief object of his ambition will be some desired place in the thought of the others, and he will feel allegiance to common standards of service and fair play....

Primary groups are primary in the sense that they give the individual his earliest and completest experience of social unity, and also in the sense that they do not change in the same degree as more elaborate relations, but form a comparatively permanent source out of which the latter are ever springing....

These groups, then, are springs of life, not only for the individual but for social institutions. They are only in part moulded by special traditions, and in larger degree express a universal nature. The religion or government of other civilizations may seem alien to us, but the children or the family group wear the common life, and with them we can always make ourselves at home.[2]

In these lines Cooley not only describes the essential features of primary group relationships but also suggests something of their functions for society as a whole. The passage exemplifies and helps define the sense in which the sociological tradition understands societies as groups.

The Secondary Group. The characteristics of the secondary group are the opposite or complement of those of the primary group. Relations among members are "cool," impersonal, rational, contractual, and formal. People participate not as whole personalities but only in delimited and special capacities; the group is not an end in itself but a means to other ends. Secondary groups are typically large and members have usually only intermittent contacts, often indirectly through the written rather than the spoken word. Examples range from the professional association to the large bureaucratic corporation to the national state itself.

Some Similar Distinctions. The sociological literature reveals a number of terms analogous to the primary/secondary distinction. Perhaps the most famous example is that of the German sociologist Ferdinand Tönnies, who developed a life's work around the dichotomy of *Gemeinschaft* and *Gesellschaft,* or as they are usually translated, community and society (or association). An English jurist, Sir Henry Maine, made a parallel distinction when he described societies of status (*Gemeinschaft,* primary) and societies of contract (*Gesellschaft,* secondary). Robert Redfield, an American anthropologist, has differentiated two types of society which he calls "folk society" (*Gemeinschaft*) and "urban society" (*Gesellschaft*).* There is no need to multiply examples: some writers have been content to employ whatever terms are in current use, while others have sought special emphases or refinements in new sets of labels. In any case, the difference exemplified by the contrast between a communal peasant life and an impersonal modern city life has been of central importance in most sociological thinking for almost as long as there has been anything called sociology.

Internal

The second approach to the study of groups may be referred to as the "internal" focus on groups as societies. This is a newer, experimentally minded tradition and derives from psychology more than from sociology. Groups are conceived of as worth studying because they are relevant environments for individual behavior—they are the subsocieties in which social interaction and the individual's part in it can be observed and tested. To be sure, the problems studied and methods used show considerable range and variation. At one extreme are those who conceive of the group as simply "others," a sort of social backdrop against which individual performance is assessed. At the other extreme are those who are scarcely concerned with the personality of the

*All these distinctions constitute "ideal types" and should be thought of as attempts to abstract out certain basic tendencies in social life. Actual social relationships are likely to be a mixture of two or more such types.

individual except as a unit or actor in a complex system of interaction—that is, in a small-scale but complicated social structure or in a network of communication.

Characteristically, the groups-as-societies approach does not concern itself with the relation of the groups studied to the society as a whole; nor is it concerned with the fact that actual individuals (as distinguished from experimental subjects) are members of many groups. The fact that this approach typically involves the use of a laboratory setting makes it very unlikely that such matters would come under direct observation.

In sum, then, the *external* approach focuses on the role of the group in X (where X, for example, equals society, the church, or the life of the individual) while the *internal* approach focuses on the role of X (where X equals something such as sentiments or communication patterns) in the life of the group.

DEFINING THE GROUP

One definition of the term *group*, which makes up in realism what it lacks in precision, was offered more than sixty years ago by one of the founders of American sociology, Albion Small. With a genial disdain for earnest hair-splitting, Small wrote:

> The term "group" serves as a convenient sociological designation for any number of people, larger or smaller, between whom such relations are discovered that they must be thought of together . . . a number of persons whose relations to each other are sufficiently impressive to demand attention.[3]

This conception of group does not, of course, distinguish between a crowd, a family, a social class, a union, and a fraternity or sorority. Some writers *have* used the term in all these senses without bothering very much about internal distinctions, but in order to make *group* a reasonably useful term a modifier must be appended to Small's definition.

Group, in the sense employed in this study, is to be distinguished from *aggregate* or *class*. To assign persons (or things, for that matter) to categories or classes or types on the basis of some common characteristic such as age, sex, or political party affiliation is, as the saying goes, to "group" them. It is quite clear, however, that the result is something other than a family or friendship group. In the first-mentioned use of the term, individuals are put together "on paper"; in the latter case there is interaction among persons and an awareness of their common membership.

Neither physical adjacency nor common interest make a group. A handful of persons standing outside the tiger cage at the zoo do not constitute a group in our sense: they are an audience having a common interest and being physically adjacent, but they are not in contact with one another. Should the tiger suddenly escape and the handful of spectators find themselves trapped inside a nearby refreshment stand, they might well *become* a group insofar as they were aware of a common fear and as they coordinated their activities in barricading doors, quieting screaming children, and so forth.

A group, then, may be defined as a plurality of individuals who are in contact with one another, who take one another into account, and who are aware of some significant commonality.

An essential feature of a group is that its members have something in common and that they believe what they have in common makes a difference. Members of one group may be aware intellectually that they all happen to be of the same sex, but this commonality makes no difference to them; it is not the basis for their group formation. Another group may have as one of its main bonds the fact of common sex—as in men's clubs in both primitive and modern society. Again, two groups may each share a common ancestor, but in one group nobody much cares while the other conceives of itself as a clan possessing the strongest imaginable source of common loyalty. Interests, beliefs, tasks, territory—all these qualities and many more may be sources of significant and meaningful ties for groups. Some groups will have but one recognized commonality; others will have many. Some groups will exhibit strong degrees of mutual attachment (families, sectarian communes, and other primary groups), while others will be held together by only the most tepid ties. Still others will find their bond of union in rational calculations of mutual advantage.

It is clear that, even without acknowledging other dimensions of group life, one can derive a large number of types of groups by the permutations and combinations of the above characteristics. Here, as in other areas, complex typologies are not difficult to create. But to be useful, a typology ought not to be cumbersome; the elaboration of distinctions and possibilities is only a part of the task of the would-be scientist. In this study the authors will forgo many refinements and will try to introduce only those distinctions necessary for the understanding of the particular problems and schools of thought under consideration.

GROUPS, SMALL AND PRIMARY

One distinction that deserves clarification at this point is between the terms *small group* and *primary group*. Except for the fact that "small" refers to numbers of members* and not to their individual sizes or their degree of affluence (as in the expression "Small Businessmen's Association") the term *small group* is a neutral, indeed a colorless, one. This is both its advantage and its shortcoming. It is an advantage in that it does not prejudge whether the group in question is operating as a primary or a secondary one. Its disadvantage is that it suggests nothing of the significance of membership either for the individual or for the society. The term *primary group* reverses these features, having the advantage of suggestiveness and the disadvantage of obscuring the possibility of secondary relations within the group.

Small and *primary*, then, are only rough equivalents, and their

---

*While it is a fruitless task to try to define a small group in terms of numbers, we may suppose that approximately twenty persons represents the upper limit of small-group size, with two being the lower limit. One of the few students of groups ever to have demonstrated a light touch calculated that the optimally efficient size of a *small* small group was .7 of a person. See Bruce Olds, "On the Mathematics of Committees, Boards and Panels," *Scientific Monthly* 63 (August 1946).

interchangeability, so widely practiced by social scientists, should be subject to a few restrictions. If one wishes to stress the importance of certain sorts of feelings and relationships among members of little groups in big organizations, the term *primary* may be desirable. The groups are small ones, to be sure, but more than merely small. If, on the other hand, one wishes to study a small-scale system of interaction and seeks to avoid the predetermination of the qualities of its internal relations, *small* is a better term. In short, *small* is the more general term for our purposes. Most primary groups are small (except for monasteries and similar communities where large numbers of persons live, presumably, in intimacy and brotherhood), but not all small groups are primary. Small groups, and especially the ad hoc laboratory ones made up of volunteers set to work solving puzzles by a professor, are likely to exhibit a general courtesy in their relations but not the loyalty and solidarity characteristic of true primary relations. Since we are interested in *all* sorts of internal group relations, the term *small group* has been used in the title and will continue to be employed throughout except where the subject matter dictates the use of *primary*.

THE ORGANIZATION OF THIS STUDY

Of the three major axes of organization of this study, two have already been introduced. The first of these was the distinction between the two traditions of group study, the external focus on societies as groups and the internal focus on groups as societies. Chapter 4 adopts the former perspective while subsequent chapters adopt the latter. The second basis for organization is the distinction between primary and secondary groups, or as it will be described later, between the "affective" and the "instrumental" aspects of group life. Finally, the three-way distinction between personality, culture, and social structure provides the third axis for the organization of this study; Chapters 5, 6, and 7, respectively, are differentiated on this basis.

Before examining the material in the light of these distinctions,

chapter three

GROUP BEHAVIOR: SOME CASE STUDIES

The case histories presented in this chapter are drawn from a variety of contexts. Taken together, they should indicate something of the range of behavior found in groups as well as something of the different approaches adopted in the study of groups. In this latter connection, it seems appropriate to describe briefly the circumstances of each study and the line of research which it embodied or engendered. Thus we will be concerned not alone with descriptions of how people in groups were seen to behave but also with how it happened that observers were there to see them.

THE INDUSTRIAL WORK GROUP

Of all the case histories familiar to students of small groups, perhaps the most frequently and fondly cited are those known collectively as the "Hawthorne" or "Western Electric" studies. This series of experiments with work groups in industry was undertaken during the late 1920s and early 30s at the Western Electric Company's Hawthorne plant in Chicago. The managers who initiated these studies were primarily interested in discovering the working conditions most conducive to increased productivity among employees doing assembly work. Some years earlier, during World War I, a number of industries had sought to increase output by rearranging rest periods. The enemy being pursued at that time was "fatigue"—that is, a physiological condition which was presumably influenced by the physical conditions of work. In the Western Electric experiments, the problem was no longer fatigue, conceived as a physiological condition, but the broader phenomenon of monotony in work, and even more inclusively, the problem of incentives.

The Relay Assembly Room

In a new program of research, the Western Electric investigators decided to introduce various wage incentive plans as variables, in addition to the older variables of work space and lighting conditions. By combining and recombining incentive schemes and working conditions they hoped to discover the most efficient and productive work arrangements. Six women whose job at the company was to assemble electrical relays were put in a special observation room (which became known as the Relay Assembly Room) and were subjected to various experimental conditions. In order to create "realistic" and "natural" conditions, the women were urged, in the words of the supervisor, "to work at a comfortable pace, and under no circumstances to try to make a race out of the test."

It was found that regardless of the presence or absence of the variables which were presumed to affect productivity, the output of the six women continued to rise over the two-year period of the experiment. This finding paralleled the results of an earlier study on the effect of illumination on productivity in which output records had been kept for alternating periods of high and of low illumination. Productivity had risen during the increased illumination stage—as had been predicted—but contrary to expectation, it had remained high even though the illumination was turned so low that it approximated bright moonlight. The patent facts of worker behavior were in direct contradiction to the common-sense expectations as to what that behavior would be. In both the illumination and the Relay Assembly Room experiments, workers continued to work harder than they should have according to management's theories of worker motivation.

The explanation for this anomalous behavior is not hard to find: the psychological conditions of work had improved. The Relay Assembly Room women thought that working in the experimental room was more fun; the supervision did not seem to them to be as constant or as onerous; they knew that the eyes of the company were upon them. The women might have felt this way if, while left in separate parts of the plant, they had been notified that they were part of a great experiment; it is conceivable that this knowledge alone might have sufficed to improve their morale and raise their output. It seems highly unlikely, however, that lasting increases in productivity could have come about without an additional stimulus. This was provided by the interaction with others in a primary group. Though the work itself consisted of operations performed as individuals rather than by teams, the women were in effect working together as members of a tiny society, a social organization having its own rules and norms of conduct, its own leadership, and its own morale and common purpose. The existence of these new *social* forces served to enhance the favorable reaction of the individual operators to the experimental situation and to create new drives to increased output.[1]

The Bank Wiring Observation Room

A subsequent experiment at the Western Electric plant took place in what is known as the Bank Wiring Observation Room —the name deriving from the fact that wires were attached and soldered in rows or banks to a telephone switchboard component. In this case, the work process was more complicated, involving several skilled and semiskilled workmen in a cooperative task. More complicated mechanically, it called for a more complex form of social interaction among the wire men, solder men, inspectors, and foremen. The working environment in this experiment was also different from that of the earlier Relay Assembly study in that the attempt was made to retain the ordinary factory arrangements and atmosphere in the experimental room. Fourteen workers and an observer were transferred into this special room. The observer sat quietly at a desk in the back of the room, ostensibly to keep records but in fact having the additional job of systematically observing the workmen.*

The major experimental variable to be tested in the Bank Wiring Observation Room was a series of wage incentive schemes built around management's assumption that workmen are economically "rational." Once again, the results did not confirm the assumptions. It turned out that the workers' brand of rationality was different from management's: where management thought it logical for a person to work extra hard for extra pay bonuses, the workers under observation thought it logical not to jeopardize their jobs by demonstrating that they really could work much faster than the management's payment plan assumed. To the Western Electric sponsors this line of thinking was quite irrational, since the company had said nothing about lowering the payment per unit produced. The workers, reacting to the Depression that surrounded them—for by now it was the early thirties—concluded that to be penny-wise in the pursuit of the bonus was to be pound-foolish in working themselves out of jobs. So they played it safe and kept the level of production steady despite the incentives offered by management.

The observed outcome of the Bank Wiring Observation Room study was the *restriction of output.* As suggested above, this result could have come about through the congruent appraisals by the individual workers of how their bread was buttered. The Western Electric researchers ignored this possibility, since for them such a reaction was "nonlogical." But what was bad research

---

*Incidentally, it might be thought that having this extra man present would be enough to throw off the others and so make unreliable and invalid any conclusions reached as to how a group would ordinarily behave. The evidence from the Bank Wiring Observation Room study—and from numerous other studies wherein the scientific observer has found it necessary to station himself close by his subjects—indicates that any disturbance caused is usually temporary and minor. Unless the participants in an experiment feel they have cause to distrust and resent the whole research arrangement, they quickly forget about an observer or a recording apparatus tucked discreetly out of the way.

procedure (that is, the refusal to consider and to eliminate alternative explanations) turned out to be lucky sociology, for it allowed attention to focus on the *group* features of the work situation. The Bank Wiring Observation Room study revealed the same phenomenon as the Relay Assembly Room: the emergence of an informal social group with its special rules and obligations. Here, however, the group pressure worked not to increase productivity but to hold it constant, to meet what the workers referred to as the "bogey" or presumed output norm. This little primary group had a common code, the key points of which clearly had the effect of inducing a steady and unvarying output. A good guy—so ran the unverbalized but nonetheless real code—won't be a rate-buster. He won't work so fast that management will lower the rate for piecework and so have the workers doing more for the same pay. Second, a good guy won't be a chiseler: he'll do his share and not expect others to "carry" him (except in certain circumstances). Third, he won't be a squealer; he will protect the group code against outside interference. Finally, he won't put on airs or be a snob—that is, he will manifest in his nonwork behavior his "democratic" submission to group ideals.

While the rules making up this particular code arose from and applied to a specific group of workers at a special time and place, the Western Electric researchers uncovered phenomena of more general significance than might at first glance be supposed. Both the Relay Assembly and the Bank Wiring studies bring out certain general principles of primary-group organization:

1. People who are in continuous contact with one another, as in a group of coworkers, tend to develop an informal social organization involving patterned behavior "outside of" or "beyond" the regularities of movement and communication necessary to avoid collisions and accomplish the task. This behavior is a subtle blend of overt activity, speech, gestures, feelings, and ideas which comes to serve as an identifying badge for the "insider" as against the "outsider."

2. An important feature of this informal social organization is a group code. This code—or at least its crucial parts—is unwritten, and group members may well be unaware of how it molds

their behavior. It is not, however, automatically or universally effective, nor does it operate without coming into conflict with other tendencies and pressures. A primary-group code, moreover, prescribes the virtues of group loyalty and says, in effect: "Be one of us."

3. Within the group not everyone behaves in the same way. For various reasons, a differentiation of roles takes place: one member becomes the clown, another the taskmaster; some are leaders and others are followers; some have high prestige and others have low. An allied phenomenon was also clearly evident in the Bank Wiring Observation Room—the subdivision of the group into two competing cliques that differed in work habits and in status.

The importance of the Western Electric research program is not that it brought to light these social phenomena for the first time. Upon reflecting, the general conclusions listed above seem quite obvious; we have all been members of groups or cliques which might be described in such terms. More important is the way in which the conclusions were reached. They were "discovered" by prestigeful and practical people who were looking for something else. Consequently, the studies could not be dismissed as mere idle speculation or as being of no interest or applicability to "real life." Nor could the emphasis on the social organization of the small group be ascribed to the preconceptions of professional social scientists bent on proving the relevance of their discipline. All in all, these studies provide one of the neatest and clearest demonstrations available of what students of primary groups are interested in and why they think their subject matter is important.

The study of the primary group in industry has been slower to develop than might have been expected, given these auspicious beginnings. This is partly because the Western Electric study came to be identified, in the minds of managers and others who heard about it, with "human relations." The glad tidings that radiated from the Harvard Business School (which had become associated with the Western Electric research program) stressed the importance of the *human* factor in industry, the need for clear channels of communication and sympathetic understanding of the problems of others. While there was considerable talk about "the group," actual emphasis has not been on the investigation of group behavior for the purpose of uncovering new sociological principles. Rather, it has been assumed that the Western Electric studies have shown us all we really need to know about the group and that from here on out the task is either to apply known principles to particular cases or to turn our attention to the wider structures (for instance, the plant) within which small groups operate. This broadening of focus may well be more realistic and more useful from the managerial point of view than is a narrow concern for one particular group or office. From the viewpoint of the student of small-group behavior, however, this widening of scope constitutes a dilution of the relatively intense kind of analysis that had originally been applied to the Bank Wiring Observation Room.

In more recent years, the study of small-group behavior has been taken up in still another area of business life. Under some such title as "conference procedure," a few of the ideas and techniques generated in other lines of research have been applied to the committee meetings of executives themselves.[2] Whatever emerges from such studies, they do seem to mark a renewed emphasis upon the operations of specific and delimited face-to-face groups.

THE BOYS' GANG

Someone has remarked that the last creature in the world to discover water would be a fish. We often have to "get away from home" and move to unfamiliar contexts in order to appreciate the significance of something we could have discovered—had we been alerted—right in our own backyards. The discovery of the group inside the Western Electric plant is a case in point. Another instance is provided by the study of the juvenile gang in the urban slum. In both cases the original interest lay in other problems—in productivity or in social amelioration—and only as the research developed did the investigators come to recognize the role of the primary group.

Chicago

One of the earliest students of the juvenile gang was Frederic Thrasher. Describing boys' gangs in Chicago slums in the 1920s, Thrasher wrote: "The gang is a primary group . . . [It] displays practically every type of corporate behavior even to the coolest deliberation and planning. Furthermore, it may develop an elaborate tradition, almost a culture of its own, and in this sense it is . . . like a society in miniature. . . ."[3] The gangs studied by Thrasher were mostly small in size: 895 of them (out of 1,100 studied) had fewer than twenty members, and the larger ones were either federations or clubs, with the original gang serving as a dominating inner circle. Even the ordinary-size gang was found to have subgroups or cliques which Thrasher described as "embryonic gang(s)." The reason for this tendency toward limited size and toward the internal division of groups into smaller cliques lies in the crucial importance of face-to-face relationships among members and the accompanying psychological closeness that is one of the chief functions of the group for its participants.

Of the internal organization of the typical gang, Thrasher writes:

> Every member of a gang tends to have a definite status within the group. Common enterprises require a division of labor. Successful conflict [with other gangs, the police, or the community in general] necessitates a certain amount of leadership, unreflective though it may be, and a consequent subordination and discipline of members. As the gang develops complex activities, the positions of individuals within the group are defined and social roles become more sharply differentiated.[4]

Thrasher goes on to mention some of the special roles which may emerge in the gang—the brains, the jester, the sissy, the show-off, the goat[5]—and to characterize the phenomenon of leadership. Of the natural leader he says, "He leads. He goes where others fear to go . . . the rest feel secure in his presence." In addition to this trait of "gameness," the leader tends to possess physical prowess, quickness and firmness of decision, imagination, and often some special knowledge, experience, or equipment (for example, a car). "In some cases," he writes, "leadership is actually diffused among a number of strong 'personalities' who share the honors and responsibilities." This condition may come about through the rise of strong lieutenants and the consequent diffusion of central command, or it may arise through the integration of supplementary strengths of members. Or, as a variation on this practice of collective leadership, there may be a rotation of leadership relative to the aims or tasks of the group.[6]

The unity of the group is not a simple matter that can be taken for granted. Except in special and temporary circumstances, Thrasher implies, domination by a leader is not an adequate explanation for the gang's cohesion. There is a form of "democracy" in the gang, and the leader "must in a very real sense accommodate himself to the wishes of the rest of the gang."[7] Those leaders who make mistakes lose their power; hence there are frequent changes in leadership in the gangs.

The group has a common code, a culture with appropriate norms and symbols, that makes for consensus; the fighting that is frequently resorted to as a means of settling differences takes place within the rules set down by this group code. It is interesting that in citing the means by which social control is established and maintained, Thrasher puts coercion and physical punishment as second only to "group opinion."[8] While the importance of violence may reflect the special conditions found in often-delinquent youth gangs, it suggests that in other kinds of groups some form of coercion—less physical no doubt, but still coercion—may play an important part in group cohesion. Allegiance voluntarily given is perhaps more of an ideal than an actuality in many cases, and laboratory experiments with groups of volunteers may overlook this possibility. If so, it is at the peril of misunderstanding group behavior.

Boston

In the 1930s, a study by William Foote Whyte of the Italian community in Boston's North End carried further many of the themes developed by Thrasher. Standing out with especial clarity in Whyte's book *Street Corner Society* is the role of the gang in the life of underprivileged boys.[9] Where Thrasher went about his investigation extensively, using reports from the police, settlement house officials, and former gang members, Whyte made an intensive study of only a few gangs and was himself a participant-observer. The result is a detailed and first-hand account of "Cornerville" life in general and of a group known as "The Nortons" or "Doc's boys" in particular.

The Internal Structure of the Group. Whyte's description makes it clear that the Nortons were a differentiated group in which individuals of different capacities and statuses were bound together in a common unity. Members formed a well understood and fairly stable hierarchy, from the peripheral members on the bottom to "Doc" at the top.[10] The activities in which the group engaged reflected this power structure: not only did the group usually do the things the leader suggested, but each member's behavior tended to be a function of his position in the group. Whyte describes how the members' bowling scores reflected not only their innate skill but also their social standing. When one skilled but low-ranking member challenged a high-ranking member to a bowling match, other group members exerted enough pressure (through razzing and other more subtle means) to make the challenger come out low scorer for the evening.

More broadly, Whyte was interested in how the group arrived at its decisions—that is, in the patterns of influence which characterized the group. Beneath the casual and seemingly random surface activity, Whyte detected fairly consistent patterns of communication: remarks traveled "up" the hierarchy during the planning of group activities, and when a decision had been reached at the top, flowed "down" to the lower ranks. The give-and-take was far more complex than a simple case of leaders telling followers what to do: each "rank" tended to interact with the rank adjacent to it, resulting in a pattern which, though more informal, resembled the chain-of-command communication flow in a bureaucracy.

Whyte further characterizes the role of the group leader in the following terms:

The leader spends more money on his followers than they on him. The farther down the structure one looks, the fewer are the financial relations which tend to obligate the leader to a follower.... The leader refrains from putting himself under obligations to those with low status in the group.

The leader is the focal point for the organization of his group. In his absence, the members of the gang are divided into a number of small groups. There is no common activity or general conversation. When the leader appears ... [he] becomes the central point in the discussion. A follower starts to say something, pauses when he notices that the leader is not listening, and begins again when he has the leader's attention....

The leader is the man who acts when the situation requires action. He is more resourceful than his followers. Past events have shown that his ideas are right. In this sense "right" simply means satisfactory to the members. He is the most independent in judgment....

When he gives his word to one of his boys, he keeps it. The followers look to him for advice and encouragement, and he receives more of their confidences than any other man. Consequently, he knows more about what is going on in the group than anyone else....

The leader is respected for his fair-mindedness. Whereas there may be hard feelings among some of the followers, the leader cannot bear a grudge against any man in the group. He has close friends (men who stand next to him in position), and he is indifferent to some of the members; but if he is to retain his reputation for impartiality, he cannot allow personal animus to override his judgment....

The leader does not deal with his followers as an undifferentiated group.... [He] mobilizes the group by dealing first with his lieutenant....

The leadership is changed not through an uprising of the bottom men but by a shift in the relations between men at the top of the structure. When a gang breaks into two parts, the explanation is to be found in a conflict between the leader and one of his former lieutenants.[11]

Individual Mobility and the Group.   In addition to the internal structure of the group, Whyte is also concerned with the effect of group membership on the individual's social mobility within the community's system of stratification. This is partly a matter of the relationship between position in the group and position in the community: the group leader is more widely known than his followers and consequently, as Whyte writes, "his capacity for social movement is greater."[12] Mobility is also, however, affected by the nature of the group itself and by the norms which it exhibits. Membership in a primary group, with its mutual loyalties and common activities and attitudes, may act as an anchor on the individual and prevent his becoming upwardly mobile and making a "success" of himself. This point is exemplified by the comparison of Doc's Nortons with the Italian Community Club headed by Chick Morelli.

Doc's boys were, in a loose sense, a gang.* Often aimless and bored, they hung around the candy shops and bowling alleys, trying to turn the many empty moments Depression unemployment granted them into mutually satisfying experiences. The group was for them an end in itself, more important than family or career.†

The Italian Community Club was a different sort of group, with different purposes and different consequences for the mobility aspirations of its members. It was a more formal organization, a secondary group, an association. It had elected officers and a set of by-laws, and its members voted by secret ballot. The official aim of the group was the improvement of the community; this purpose was not, however, thought of by members as necessarily being opposed to improvement and advancement of the individual club member.[13] The club was a voluntary association of the sort so common in middle-class suburbia. To refer to it as a "gang" would be, in a club member's opinion, the final insult.

---

*Since Whyte wanted his reader to approach his subjects as human beings caught in an unpromising environment, he does not often use the term "gang," with its connotations of tough guys and mayhem.

†"Home plays a very small role in the group activities of the corner boy. Except when he eats, sleeps, or is sick, he is rarely at home, and his friends always go to his corner first when they want to find him ... married or single, the corner boy can be found on his corner almost every night of the week." Street Corner Society, p. 255.

The Italian Community Club was a means to an end—improvement for self and society—while the Norton Gang was an end in itself. The former inculcated the ideals of self-help, independence, and success, and taught skills necessary to social ascent; the latter emphasized mutual loyalty and responsibility and did little to prepare members for anything except continued membership. In a sense, both groups taught individuals how to get along with others, but who the "others" were and what "getting along" meant were quite different in the two cases. This polariy is reflected in the two leaders, Chick and Doc. Chick was a go-getter; Doc was not. Chick broke away sufficiently from community and age-mates to go to college and law school; Doc remained one of the boys. Chick was socially mobile and a success; Doc remained a nice guy.

The group itself (here and elsewhere) is not an original cause, an unmoved mover; its existence does not "explain" ethnic minority relations, slums, or social mobility. Nevertheless, without knowledge of the ways in which the individual relates himself to his group—to a whole series of groups throughout his lifetime —one is scarcely in a position to understand, let alone change, the patterns of social behavior as they are found on the street corners of the city slum.[14]

DEMOCRATIC, LAISSEZ-FAIRE, AND AUTHORITARIAN GROUPS

The small-group research described so far in this chapter was carried out by people who were trained in or interested in sociology. They were intent upon studying the small group as it is found in real-life situations, in industry and among the underprivileged. Let us look now at a study carried on by social psychologists. The particular individuals who undertook this research were, like their sociologist cousins, very much concerned with broad-scale social problems, but they hoped to get at these problems by the use of laboratory methods. Under controlled conditions, group activity could be varied systematically and could be observed in terms of relatively precise categories.

Such procedures, they felt, would yield generalizations about the effect of specific variables on group behavior, and these generalizations would be relevant to our understanding of broader social problems.

The study in question was done by Ronald Lippitt and Ralph White under the guidance of the distinguished Gestalt psychologist Kurt Lewin. The social and political problem with which the authors were concerned was the effect of "democratic," "authoritarian," and "laissez-faire" styles of leadership on the behavior of groups.[15] The objectives of the study, in the words of the authors, were

> 1. To study the effects on group and individual behavior of three experimental variations in adult leadership in four clubs of eleven-year-old children. These three styles may be roughly labeled as "democratic," "authoritarian," and "laissez-faire."

> 2. To study the group and individual reactions to shifts from one type of leadership to another within the same group.

> 3. To seek relationships between the nature and content of other group memberships, particularly the classroom and family, and the reactions to the experimental social climates.

> 4. To explore the methodological problems of setting up comparative "group test situations," to develop adequate techniques of group process recording, and to discover the degree to which experimental conditions could be controlled and manipulated within the range of acceptance by the group members.[16]

The research procedure designed to fulfill these objectives involved the creation of activity clubs of five youngsters each, matched for such characteristics as IQ, popularity, physical energy, and leadership. The children were set to work on craft projects under the direction of adult leaders who had been thoroughly briefed as to the three styles of leadership they were to adopt. Leaders were rotated among the groups, each leader adopting each role, so that the effect of the individual leader's personality as such would be, so to speak, randomized.

In the *authoritarian* role, the adult leader was strongly directive, taking primary responsibility for assigning tasks and working companions, and indicating as the need arose the steps to be followed (rather than outlining the total plan ahead of time). He praised or condemned the children's work arbitrarily and did not give reasons why he thought something good or bad. He was aloof from the group, demonstrated rather than participated, and gave frequent orders and commands. In the *democratic* role, group discussion and decision was encouraged by the leader. He tried to outline the steps necessary to reach the group's goals and to suggest alternative approaches. He left the children to work as they pleased and remained objective and "fact-minded" in his criticism and praise. He was the most willing of three types of leaders to joke, to discuss nonclub activities, and in general to put himself on the same level as his charges. Finally, in the *laissez-faire* role, the leader played a much more passive part than in the other two. He gave the group almost complete freedom to do as it wished, standing ready to help if asked for assistance but making very few suggestions. He was friendly rather than stand-offish, but did not attempt "to evaluate negatively or positively the behavior or productions of the individuals or the group as a group. . . ."[17]

The observation of the activity in the several groups was far more detailed than anything attempted by Thrasher or Whyte. Four observers, peering through peepholes, recorded group activity and conversation. Motion pictures were made so that the researchers, and posterity, might seek at their leisure evidence of sociological and psychological principles.

It was found that each of the three styles of leadership called forth clearly distinguishable styles of group behavior. When the groups were under *democratic* leadership, relations among members were more personal and friendly. More individual differences were shown, and yet at the same time members were more "group-minded" and looked to one another for mutual approval. There was less scapegoating in the democratic groups and a steadier level of work when the leader was (by design) out of the room.

The same groups under *laissez-faire* leadership were notable for their lack of achievement. They asked more questions of the leader but lacked "the social techniques necessary for group decision and cooperative planning." Lippitt and White find it suggestive that "two or three times . . . when the adult left, one of the boys exerted a more powerful leadership and achieved a more coordinated group activity than when the relatively passive adult was present."[18]

Authoritarian leadership evoked two patterns of reaction, one "aggressive" and the other "apathetic." Both reactions shared a relatively strong dependence on the leader, but the aggressive reaction involved a rebelliousness and demanding of attention, and a mutual friendliness among members, which were lacking in the apathetic groups. The presence of internal solidarity rather than scapegoating in the aggressive authoritarian groups is ascribed by Lippitt and White to the group's ability to

> focus its aggression sufficiently in other channels (toward the leader and toward the out-group) so that in-group tension did not rise to a dangerously high point. . . . The underlying spirit of rebellion toward the leader and cooperation in out-group aggression seem to be the "cohesive forces" in aggressive autocracy, while in apathetic autocracy with its lower level of felt frustration, the shared submissiveness seemed to do away with all incentive to competition for social status.[19]

When the group leadership changed from authoritarian to democratic or laissez-faire, the previously apathetic groups indulged in "great outbursts of horseplay between the members."[20] With regard to emotional freedom and "letting off steam," the authors conclude that "the adult restrictiveness of the benevolent authoritarian role and the environmental unstructuredness of the laissez-faire situation were both found to inhibit greatly genuine 'psychological freedom' as contrasted to 'objective freedom.' "[21] Thus the authors were able to arrive at the conclusion that social-psychological investigation of groups supports progressive democratic values.

The Lippitt and White study, undertaken during the 1930s, perhaps strikes us today as more consciously ideological than does most contemporary small-group research. In social science, as elsewhere, mood and fashion have changed. It may be appropriate, however, to note that the group-atmosphere study, despite its tendency to identify small-scale helpfulness with large-scale politics, had the virtue of concerning itself with questions that mattered. It is for this reason, as well as for its groundbreaking experimental techniques, that the Lippitt and White study is a landmark in the study of group behavior.

INTERPERSONAL ATTRACTION

The last study that we will treat in some detail was also conducted by a social psychologist. In this case, Theodore M. Newcomb, a professor of social psychology at the University of Michigan, was interested in both interpersonal attraction and the ways in which individuals seem to strive for balance in interpersonal relations. He noted that individuals who are strangers to one another will, under conditions assuring that they will become well acquainted, experience many changes in the degree of their attraction toward one another. Such changes presumably occur in orderly ways.

To test his hypotheses and to gain more insight into the attraction process Newcomb arranged to have a large house near the university furnished as a living unit for men.[22] During two successive years a set of seventeen men who had transferred from other universities were provided with room and board in exchange for allowing themselves to be observed and tested as they went about getting acquainted. They were selected as total strangers to one another. For sixteen weeks they lived and took their meals together in the house reserved for them. Each week they responded to a selected set of questionnaires, attitude scales, and other tests, many of which were repeated from time to time. In particular, they rated or ranked each other on attraction during almost every week. In addition, they frequently estimated one another's attitudes of various kinds.

Newcomb was especially interested in whether or not the patterns of attraction and rejection between individuals would exist in "balanced states." He wished to test the hypothesis that if there was not initially a balanced state, then there would be a tendency to change toward balance. If this change was not possible, then the state of imbalance would produce tension. He expected that individuals' attraction to the remaining group members would at first be unstable, because initial attraction responses (made on the third day) are necessarily based upon first impressions only; and that week-to-week changes should be in the direction of increased stability—that is, that the rate of change will be a declining one, because in successive weeks the amount of "new" information that individuals receive about one another will decline. The kinds of information about another person that are relevant to attraction toward that person are, in general, those that result in the attribution to the person of properties that are regarded as rewarding. These are not necessarily persistent or "inherent" personal traits; they may equally well include properties that are elicited only in interaction with specific other persons, and they may, of course, be idiosyncratically attributed. Changes in attraction result not only from new discoveries of what characteristics another person already has, but also from observing qualities that, whether one knows it or not, one has oneself helped elicit in the person.

Newcomb's analysis of the ratings of attraction supported both predictions. The initial responses had little predictive value even for so short a period as five weeks. Change continued throughout the entire period, but the rate of change declined hardly at all after the first five or six weeks. An exception was found in the very unpopular subjects whose high-attraction choices were not reciprocated and continued to be relatively erratic.

Also as expected there was an almost universal tendency to assume that one's two most preferred choices are highly attracted toward each other. That is, the subjects perceived that triads were almost perfectly balanced. It seemed to be almost unthinkable to the subjects that their most-preferred choices should be hostile to each other or even merely "neutral." The subjects also perceived agreement with attractive others about objects other than the self and the house members.

Once high-attraction pairs were formed, they tended to take

in another member. These triads in turn were likely to prove highly attractive to others. By the time the subjects had given their final ratings of attraction the structures of attraction for the two house groups appeared as they are presented in the sociograms in Figure 1. The circles represent individuals and the connecting lines represent mutual attraction at high levels. The two group structures did not differ in important ways at first, but interesting difference appeared later as shown in Figure 1. The visual appearance of the two sociograms, together with certain other evidence, suggested differences along a dimension that Newcomb called centrality versus divisiveness—a difference that he had not predicted. There seemed to be two variables involved in centrality. One was the degree of interconnectedness among high mutual attraction dyads on the part of the individuals having the highest attraction power (popularity). The second variable was the amount of attraction power concentrated in these individuals. It was found that among the most popular six individuals in each group, who together accounted for somewhat more than half of the attraction power in each group, 20 percent of all such dyads met the criterion of interconnectedness in the first year of the study as compared with 53 percent in the second. Moreover, there was more attraction power concentrated in the six most popular individuals in the second year than in the first. Following the experiment Newcomb concluded that the reason why there were so many more persons involved in multiple interconnections in the second year was simply that there was more agreement among the six popular individuals.

With regard to the individual characteristics of the subjects, the tendencies to be sensitive to balanced relationships and to judge others' attitudes more accurately with increasing acquaintance appeared to be present, at least in some degree, in all of the subjects.

Nature of Constant Relations

Newcomb summarizes his findings by noting that three kinds of elements had been considered in the study: (1) an individual's attraction toward another person; (2) an individual's attitude to-

Year I, Week 15

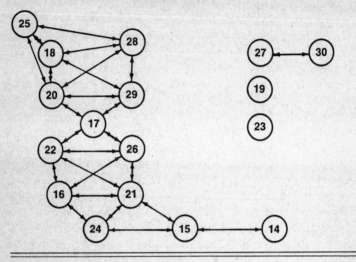

Year II, Week 15

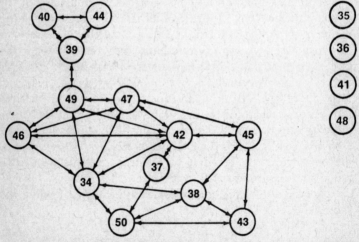

FIGURE 1. High-attraction structure of two populations on final acquaintance. Circles represent individuals; connecting lines represent mutual attraction at high levels.

Source: Theodore M. Newcomb, *The Acquaintance Process.* (New York: Holt, Rinehart and Winston, 1961), pp. 172, 173. Reprinted by permission.

ward some object other than that person; and (3) that person's attitude, as the individual perceives it, toward the same object. For the two sets of university undergraduates in this study the stability curves of these three kinds of elements were quite different. Attitudes toward nonperson objects (especially toward general values) showed little change from first to last acquaintance. Attraction toward other house members, on the part of most subjects, became relatively stable by the end of the first six weeks or so. The estimates of others' attitudes were relatively slow in stabilizing, though with individual differences. Thus if the study had been concerned only with subjects' own attitudes and attractions, it might well have been terminated after six rather than sixteen weeks. But given the relatively slow and continuing changes in estimates of others' attitudes, it might well have continued for another several weeks. Despite the continuing changes, balanced relationships between all types of objects were found at all stages of acquaintance.

Thus individuals in any situation prefer relationships that are balanced and tend to adapt to information regarded as valid. Sets of individuals also tend to make successive adaptations to each other in order to establish relationships that are both realistic and balance-promoting for each individual.

OTHER SOURCES OF INTEREST IN THE SMALL GROUP

Before leaving this account of varieties of interest in group behavior, it is instructive to examine briefly the interest in small groups in some other contexts.

The Military

The importance of the small or primary group in the operation of military forces has received considerable attention. The material gathered for the multivolume study *The American Soldier* throws a good deal of light on the functions of primary groups in the United States Army during World War II.[23] A subsequent article by Edward Shils pulls this material together and presents certain conclusions about the role of the small unit within the larger military organization.[24] These conclusions are worth citing.

It is fairly clear that when it came to maintaining his courage under fire, the average American soldier in World War II was not sustained by either his patriotic ideals or his hatred of the enemy. Rather, it was loyalty to his particular outfit and the primary relationships with his fellow targets that did the most to strengthen the combat soldier's morale. The primary group, say the authors of *The American Soldier*, "served two principal functions in combat motivation: it set and emphasized group standards of behavior and it supported and sustained the individual in stresses he would otherwise not have been able to withstand."[25] Clearly, this does not mean that the formal military bureaucracy plays only a minor role in getting soldiers to fight. Among the many functions performed by the formal organization is the setting of the goals of the primary groups from which individual soldiers draw their strength. As Shils observes, "efforts to achieve the . . . formally prescribed goals may be strengthened by [primary group] membership."[26] Similar conclusions concerning the role of primary-group membership are also revealed by studies of the United States Air Force and of the German army during World War II.[27]

Opinion Research

Public-opinion polling is probably the most familiar application of social science in contemporary America. Some of its developments bring it very close to the field of small-group research.

To many persons, polling is a practical, if sometimes inaccurate, technique for predicting elections and counting the public pulse on various issues of the day. In the advertising and marketing worlds, the pollster has secured a prominent place for himself by providing manufacturers and advertising agencies with information about the public reaction to changes in product design, packaging, and other aspects of selling goods and services. This tremendous public and commercial interest in trying to figure out whether people prefer this soap or that candidate has tended to obscure the scientific and theoretical problems in opinion research. In the last two decades sociologists, psychologists, and others interested in opinion research have begun to explore systematically the relevance to their special field of the findings and insights of the other social sciences. Or, to put it somewhat differently, some opinion research people have redefined their own focus so that it is no longer simply a question of whether a public act or statement changes people's attitudes or behavior, but more broadly, how people make up their minds. Paul Lazarsfeld and Elihu Katz have described this development as follows: "... mass media research has aimed at an understanding of how, and under what conditions, mass media 'campaigns' (rather specific, short-run efforts) succeed in influencing opinions and attitudes...." The basic assumption of such research, they continue, has been that of "the omnipotent media, on one hand, sending forth the message, and the atomized masses, on the other, waiting to receive it—and nothing in-between."[28]

These authors proposed that opinion research concern itself with more factors than the message on the one end and the polled respondent on the other. It should also focus on the more long-range public symbols and events and on the process by which the interpretation of these events and symbols is developed and transmitted among the public. This public, in turn, should not be seen simply as a mass of individuals, but (as we in fact know it to be by personal experience as well as by scientific study) as a highly complex set of interlocking and overlapping groups.

> No longer [they write] can mass media research be content with a random sample of disconnected individuals as respondents. Respondents must be studied within the context of the group or groups to which they belong or which they have "in mind"— thus, which may influence them—in their formulation of opinions, attitudes or decisions, and in their rejection or acceptance of mass media in influence-attempts.[29]

So important is the study of these groups, in the opinion of Katz and Lazarsfeld, that they preface their empirical study of the flow of influence in a Midwestern community with a 134-page review of small-group research. A major portion of this review deals with what they call the "rediscovery of the primary group" in various fields of social science; they conclude that "it was not simply the fact that the primary group *exists* that was discovered, but the fact that it was *relevant* to an understanding of . . . mass production [the Western Electric studies], combat morale [*The American Soldier*], class status and mobility [*Street Corner Society*], and communications behavior."[30]

These brief references do not, of course, exhaust the list of persons who have shown an interest in the structure and functioning of small groups. There is, for example, the awareness among psychotherapists that what takes place in a group session is not simply a multiple replication of what goes on in an individual session. Or again, and in contrast to the specialized and professional interests mentioned so far, there is a very widespread interest in more effective group meetings on the part of schools, clubs, associations, conferences, programs, and all the myriad get-togethers that typify American life. This utilitarian and characteristically American passion for better techniques is perhaps the most potent impetus for much of the work being done on small groups today, but it has, for better or worse, been but inadequately reflected in these pages. The rationale for this neglect is that the intention of this chapter has not been to enumerate every possible reason why one might study the small group, but merely to suggest—by citing some better-known instances of research—something of the variety of interests in the field of small-group analysis.

chapter four

THE
FUNCTIONS
OF
GROUPS

This chapter looks at groups externally, from the outside, and in a sociological and historical fashion rather than internally, after the manner of the psychologists and experimentalists. The aim is to describe the major functions of groups, especially primary groups, for the individual, for the formal organization, and for the larger society.

GROUP FUNCTIONS FOR THE INDIVIDUAL

Functions of the Primary Group

What does the group—that is, the fact of membership in the group—"do" for the individual?

We can begin at the most common-sense level and say that being a member of a primary group is fun. This is to say, in less colloquial terms, that the group provides affective satisfactions or personal response, that it brings psychic gratification or enjoyment. This positive and subjective evaluation of why members like to be in their groups seems to be universal; when asked a question about what he gets out of being a member, an individual is likely to give an answer along these lines—as, for instance, did the women in the Relay Assembly Room. The generality—indeed, the obviousness—of this point once led one sociologist, W. I. Thomas, to postulate as one of the four basic human "wishes" the desire for the "response" so universally provided by the primary group.

Looking at this matter objectively—that is, through the eyes of the social scientist observer rather than subjectively through the eyes of the individual group member—we may hope to add something to the notion that groups are fun. The primary group may be said to have the associated functions of training and support.

To say that primary groups "train" members means that the group aids in the psychological development of the individual by providing the context in which his intellectual and emotional development take place. Far and away the most prominent instance of this process is to be found in that primary group known as the family.

Thanks in good part to the seminal influence of the philosopher and psychologist George Herbert Mead,[1] American social scientists have for many years been acutely conscious of this crucial role of the primary group. Mead describes how the child's personality is developed in relation to "significant others" —that is, members of the family or of other primary groups such as the play group. The child not only learns the "rules of the game" (to borrow a phrase from the Swiss psychologist Jean Piaget, whose explorations parallel at many points those of Mead), but comes to understand the very nature of selfhood. The child internalizes the attitudes of others by virtue of an ability to "take the role of the other"; in this process the objects of the child's attitudes are not only external objects but the internalizer and role-taker (that is, the child) him- or herself. Thus, the child not only learns the words by which the culture identifies things and events but also becomes aware of her- or himself as a distinct identity.

As noted earlier, Charles Horton Cooley stressed the importance of the primary group as the great socializer, the incubator of human character—human because it is social. Mead, however, carried further the logical analysis of the development of the self in the group context, and related his conclusions much more explicitly to the basic problems of philosophy and social science. We learn from Mead in what a profound sense men and women are social animals, taking not merely their surface apparel but their very psychic skeleton from the social environment in which they live and grow. But Mead was not, in the last analysis, concerned with the primary group per se; he was content to speak of "others" and "the social world" as a kind of nutrient medium in which the development of the individual takes place. This leaves us without specific descriptions of those features of group life that succeed or fail in the creation of the individual personality.

In this connection, it may be noted in passing that psychoanalysis offers an immense amount of data, and of conjecture, on many of the problems which Cooley and Mead raise. Freud and his followers went further than did Mead in specifying the consequences of different roles within the familial primary group for the child's psychological development. For psychoanalysis, it is of pivotal importance whether the "other" with whom the child interacts is father, mother, younger sister, or older brother. The concepts of Oedipal conflict or of sibling rivalry—indeed, the whole dynamic character of psychoanalysis—would disappear if such role distinctions were not made and if the family were thought of merely as a close group of culture-bearers.

At all stages of development, then, the primary group plays a vital part in the psychic life of the individual by providing him with training, support, and the opportunity for intimacy and emotional response.

To be sure, this is not a new idea. Within the sociological tradition probably the most explicit—and eloquent—statement of the general point is still the one made by Emile Durkheim, the founder of modern French sociology, some fifty years ago:

> Society is not alone in its interest in the formation of special groups ... the individual, on his part, finds joy in it, for anarchy

is painful to him. He also suffers from pain and disorder produced whenever inter-individual relations are not submitted to some regulating influence. It is not good for man to live with the threat of war in the midst of his immediate companions. This sensation of general hostility, the mutual defiance resulting from it, the tension it necessitates, are difficult states when they are chronic.... Common life is attractive as well as coercive ... when individuals who are found to have common interests associate, it is not only to defend their interests, it is to associate, that is, not to feel lost among adversaries, to have the pleasure of community, to make one out of many, which is to say, finally, to lead the same moral life together.[2]

Disfunctions of the Primary Group

Having noted the primary group's positive functions for the individual, we should also be aware of the harmful or disfunctional effects it may have. A primary group may restrict, inhibit, or even smother the individual in its close embrace. The individual, in turn, is usually impelled to resist this pressure in some measure even while welcoming the gratifications which the group affords. The balance between resistance to and acceptance of the group varies with the society, the individual, and even, so to speak, with the time of day. All of us have experienced these contradictory tendencies in our own group memberships: at the same time that we wish to belong we also wish to differentiate ourselves and to proclaim our individuality.

In our society, perhaps the most general and most acute instance of this rebellion—which is rarely a total rebellion—is the adolescent's struggle with the family. For Americans at least, the achievement of independence from the parents is aided, and in many cases even made possible, by the peer group. In other words, one primary group (a voluntary one) helps to break the emotional hold of another primary group (an involuntary one). Viewed in this way, the frantic teen-age culture of America has positive functions not only for the individual (by providing emotional leverage against parental domination), but also for the society in that it helps produce individuals who are psychologically more independent of the traditionalism which parents often represent to their children.

There are important questions of values here which the concept of "function" should not be allowed to obscure. To say that peer groups have positive functions is not to grant a scientific blessing to every activity of a teen-age gang. From a moral or from a psychiatric point of view, the family frying pan may be preferable, in some instances, to the teen-age fire. Further poignancy is added to this situation by the fact that the parties involved are often unable to distinguish between their own short-run wishes and their long-term needs; what appears functional in one of these perspectives may be disfunctional in another. The problem for the sociologist, then, when discussing functions and disfunctions, is to specify the groups that are being described and the temporal and value perspectives that are employed. This point is worth keeping in mind because some writers are prone to stress the positive functions of "the" primary group without making clear that implicit value assumptions have quietly crept into their presumably scientific generalizations.

GROUP FUNCTIONS FOR THE ORGANIZATION

When we speak of group functions for an organization, we refer to the part played by the small, and essentially primary, group within secondary groups or associations or formal organizations. This matter has been extensively treated by students of bureaucracy,[3] and we need do no more than note a few salient points.

In the first place, the literature on formal organizations or bureaucracies reveals positive and negative roles for the primary group. On the positive side, it has been frequently found that solidary bonds among coworkers are necessary for high morale and that morale is an important factor in high productivity; the case of the Relay Assembly Room women is an instance of this relationship. Membership in a primary group within the formal organization strengthens the individual in his or her sense of duty and therefore strengthens the organization; this is brought out by the authors of *The American Soldier*. Furthermore, by providing personal satisfaction outside the sphere of organizational activities—indeed, by providing a respite from organizational demands—the primary group makes it possible for the individual to return to a task with renewed energy. That these functional relationships are not merely matters of efficiency in the Purchasing Department of the ABC Corporation but also have profound significance for long-range cultural development has been amply demonstrated by the work of the German sociologists Max Weber and Ernst Troeltsch.[4]

The disfunctions of the primary group for the formal organization are readily discernible. As the Bank Wiring Observation Room study shows, to cite but one familiar example, the close-knit group may act to restrict productivity. In such a case, one would speak of the primary group as functional for the individual (insofar as it provides personal gratifications and helps make the job more secure) and disfunctional for the organization. The fact that loyalty to the primary group can lead to sabotage, buck-passing, gold-bricking, and similar consequences so colorfully recorded in our language is a matter of common observation.

Here again, as in the case of the individual's relation to the group, a more precise and yet more general analysis of the conditions under which the primary group may operate for or against the larger organization is needed. It is not enough to note that things can work either way, or perhaps most often, both ways at the same time. More research and more generalized theoretical formulations will be required before this matter can be dealt with satisfactorily.

GROUP FUNCTIONS FOR SOCIETY

To speak of the functions, both positive and negative, of the group for society is to take a broader perspective on many of the problems already raised. An observation frequently made by commentators on American society is that of the ubiquity and usefulness of special-purpose "secondary" associations. To cite only one of these observations—from the pen of that incomparable reporter and savant Alexis de Tocqueville:

> The political associations that exist in the United States are only a single feature in the midst of the immense assemblage of associations in that country. Americans of all ages, all conditions, and all dispositions, constantly form associations. They have not only commercial and manufacturing companies, in which all take part, but associations of a thousand other kinds—religious, moral, serious, futile, extensive or restricted, enormous or diminutive. The Americans make associations to give entertainments, to found establishments for education, to build inns, to construct churches, to diffuse books, to send missionaries to the antipodes; and in this manner they found hospitals, prisons, and schools. If it be proposed to advance some truth, or to foster some feeling by the encouragement of a great example, they form a society.[5]

Tocqueville recognized that the predilection for association was not a mere cultural peculiarity, akin to the American's fondness for corn likker or pumpkin pie; rather, it was closely associated with the principle of equality, which, as Tocqueville saw it, was the fundamental theme of American society. Without the ability to combine in the pursuit of common ends, a democratic and equalitarian society must either fragment and thereby stagnate, or give way to some authoritarian form. Thus Tocqueville concludes that "in democratic countries the science of association is the mother of science; the progress of all the rest depends upon the progress it has made."[6]

The Case for the Negative

Turning from the role of secondary associations in modern heterogeneous society to the role of more primary groupings, let us take up first the case for the negative—that is, the argument that primary groups and primary bonds are harmful or disfunctional for the larger society.

The fundamental notion here is that primary bonds—taking such forms as localism, communalism, and loyalty to kin—are restraints on justice and progress. The attachment of the shepherd to a clan or the peasant to a village, for example, may make it difficult or impossible for the state to mete out uniform justice or demand equal services. Our beliefs that the law should be no respecter of persons, that the punishment should fit the crime and not the criminal, and that what is asked of one should be asked of all—all eventually run up against local and primary ties. You cannot have a society where in fundamental matters people cleave to their own kith and kin and at the same time treat everybody objectively and as equals. The former emphasis may be described in terms of the principles of *particularism* and *ascription,* the latter in terms of *universalism* and *achievement.* The first pair stress the primacy of the traditional bonds of sentiment that grow up among persons sharing a common habitat or name; they stress the unifying factors which are "given" or *ascribed* without any act of volition on the part of the individual; the resulting bonds involve special or *particular* other persons. The principles of universalism and achievement embody the opposite and complementary emphases: on impersonal and abstract bases for evaluation and on the importance of *what* a person can do (achieve) rather than on *who* the person is. A belief that an individual deserves "fair" treatment regardless of color, creed, or associates is a belief in universalism and achievement. These sets of principles are by no means always as sharply opposed as the above definitions might suggest. They are, nevertheless, contrary tendencies that underlie much of the strain and controversy constantly besetting our attempts at civilization.

In the broadest historical sense, the postmedieval period has been one in which the principle of particularism has given way to the principle of universalism. Or to put it in terms that have appeared earlier in this study, there has been a transition from "community" to "society," from *Gemeinschaft* to *Gesellschaft,* from Durkheim's "mechanical" to "organic" solidarity. It has been a fundamental tendency of social thought for at least a century to think in terms of these *types* of society and of the historical transition from the one to the other.

An Illustration from the Enlightenment and Rousseau. A less generalized and more tendentious version of this line of thought characterized much of the thinking of the eighteenth-century Enlightenment. The Enlightenment attacked localism, backwardness, and traditional bonds (which were held to be associated with ignorance, error, superstition, and medievalism generally) in the name of science, reason, and humanity. Progress, it was thought, would see the replacement of traditional, local, semi-feudal, and irrational social arrangements by a universalistic social order embodying the abstract virtues of justice, sensibility, manners, and—in the view of some writers—equality.

The application of this point of view to the role of groups in society was made, though at no great length, by the political philosopher Jean Jacques Rousseau. In *The Social Contract*, Rousseau argued that autonomous local groups, associations, and (in the classic sense of the word) corporations inhibited the full and free development of both the individual and the society. In order that the individual's real freedom and society's true goal might prevail, Rousseau concluded, it would be better if such groups did not exist.[7]

It was natural enough for Rousseau to share his age's faith in what has here been called the principle of universalism, and to hold that progress meant the elimination of particularism. Rousseau departed from the other philosophers of the Enlightenment in going beyond their attacks on particular abuses or their criticism of irrationality and injustice as such, and in arguing for the abolition of all intermediary groupings that might embody particularistic holdovers. The extraordinary system of interlocking, overlapping, specially privileged, and mutually checkmating corporate entities that went to make up eighteenth-century French society (the result of what historians have called "the second feudalization of France") made the elimination of this organizational logjam an understandable goal for reformers desirous of creating a uniform national code and administration. But Rousseau was not historically specific in his discussion of these problems in *The Social Contract:* by casting the argument in its general form he both created a theoretical issue and laid the basis for the charge that he was, wittingly or unwittingly, a philosopher of totalitarianism.

The Case for the Affirmative

The fundamental criticism of Rousseau is that in exalting the idea of society (in the form of his concept of the "General Will") and by eliminating intermediating corporate groups, Rousseau leaves the individual free and unburdened only in abstract theory. In reality, the individual would stand defenseless before the power of the state. In contrast to Rousseau, most modern commentators hold that groups are *essential* to political freedom. The protection of social and political freedom is thus the chief positive function of the group for the society.

This anti-Rousseauian position has received its most cogent formulation at the hands of Emile Durkheim, the man who, quite paradoxically, draws so heavily on *The Social Contract* for much of his social theory. Durkheim writes:

> A society composed of an infinite number of unorganized individuals, that a hypertrophied State is forced to oppress and contain, constitutes a veritable sociological monstrosity.... Where the State is the only environment in which men can live communal lives, they inevitably lose contact, become detached, and thus society disintegrates. A nation can be maintained only if, between the State and the individual, there is inter-colated a whole series of secondary groups near enough to the individuals to attract them strongly in their sphere of action and drag them, in this way, into the general torrent of social life.... The absence of all corporative institution creates ... a void whose importance it is difficult to exaggerate. It is a whole system of organs necessary in the normal functioning of the common life which is wanting.... It is the general health of the social body which is here at stake.[8]

Although the nineteenth century recognized the vital political functions of groups—as is evidenced by the traditions of pluralism in England and of syndicalism in France—the idea has acquired a special urgency in the twentieth century. The rise of the totalitarian states after World War I inspired in many thinkers a harsher and more searching criticism of the liberal dogmas, in terms of which the facts of modern dictatorship seemed largely inexplicable. History and political theory were reappraised, and there was a precipitous rise in the reputation of such conservatives as Edmund Burke, a writer who in some quarters replaced Marx as the great sociologist and prophet of the nineteenth century.

Totalitarianism and the Mass Society. Contemporary sociologically oriented writing on the subject of totalitarianism and the mass society has taken over wholeheartedly the position set forth by Durkheim.[9] Observers find that modern industrial society tends, even in democratic countries, to be a "mass" society in which people are pushed, shoved, stamped, and molded into the proper combination of docility and fanaticism. Under totalitarian conditions these tendencies are made thoroughgoing actualities: the remaining primary ties to community and family are ripped asunder, the variabilities and uniquenesses of individuals and groups are brutally liquidated, and what remains is a mass of atomized robots subject to the arbitrary command of the all-powerful state.

This critique of the deracinated society is exemplified by Robert Nisbet's *The Quest for Community.* Nisbet writes that

> the ominous preoccupation with community revealed by modern thought and mass behavior is a manifestation of certain profound dislocations in the primary associative areas of society, dislocations that have been created to a great extent by the structure of the Western political State ... the problem is social— social in that it pertains to the statuses and social memberships which men hold or seek to hold. But the problem is also political —political in that it is a reflection of the present location and distribution of power in society.[10]

> [The dislocations] lie in the realm of the small, primary, personal relationships of society—the relationships that mediate directly between man and his larger world of economic, moral, and political and religious values.[11]

> [There is no real role for] the primary social group in an economy and political order whose principal ends have come to be structured in such a way that the primary social relationships are

increasingly functionless, almost irrelevant, with respect to these ends.[12]

[As a result] individuals seek escape from the freedom of impersonality, secularism, and individualism. They look for community in marriage, thus putting, often, an intolerable strain upon a tie already grown institutionally fragile. They look for it in easy religion, which leads frequently to a vulgarization of Christianity the like of which the world has not seen before. They look for it in the psychiatrist's office, in the cult, in functionless ritualizations of the past, and in all other avocations of relief from nervous exhaustion.[13]

Writers of Nisbet's persuasion hold, then, that the primary group is withering away, that its absence makes possible—indeed, likely —the growth of state tyranny, and that tyranny, once established, consolidates its position by destroying any remaining independent groups.

The relation between society and primary group may be clarified by taking a closer look at the latter concept. An essay by Edward Shils distinguishes three types of group bonds, all of which are in some sense primary.[14]

First, there is what may be called the "primordial" primary group. Tönnies had this type most clearly in mind when he described the *Gemeinschaft:* the group united by common blood or common neighborhood and exemplified by the peasant community. Membership in such a group is involuntary and produces a traditionalist outlook respectful of long-term identities not subject to rational choice or calculation.

Second, there is the "personal" primary group, distinguished by the voluntary attachment of individuals who like one another personally. It is the group of friends who can relax and enjoy themselves in one another's presence. The primary groups in the formal organizations of factory and army are predominantly of this type. Although personal ties of this sort may also arise among individuals who are thrown together and thus share a common territory, somewhat after the fashion of the primordial group, their essentially voluntary nature distinguishes the latter from the former. Propinquity is an important condition for the formation of personal primary groups, but it does not of itself entail the significance that a common habitation has for, say, villagers.

Third may be distinguished the "ideological" primary group, made up of those who share a common ideal to which they are intensely devoted. Revolutionary, chiliastic, millenarian, sectarian in their outlook, such bands are obsessed with ideas and feel themselves to be bearers of truth and virtue in a wicked world. This type of group shares with the primordial group the feeling for the "sacred" quality of their union. In the one case, it is the traditional order that calls forth awe and respect on the part of group members; in the other, it is the new order, the "cause," that is holy. Both of these types stand in contrast to the more casual and noncharismatic personal primary group. On the other hand, the personal and the ideological group share the feature of voluntariness, a feature the primordial group lacks.

The ideological primary group plays an important part in revolutionary social movements and in modern totalitarian parties. The psychological hold which the Communist party cell has for its members has frequently been noted. The strength of these nonrational bonds is attested by the agonies which defectors report when they break with their major source of security, the Communist party. Nazism relied on similar group bonds, with the difference that while Communism officially and ostensibly employs a "scientific" appeal to rational interests, Nazism was quite frank in its appeal to "supra-scientific" and nonlogical emotions of *Gemeinschaft*. An intensified version of the techniques of using primary-group bonds to break down old values was developed in China after the Korean War as part of the Chinese political reeducation program. Both civilian and military prisoners were assigned to small study groups in which they were forced—by overt and covert group pressure, as well as by individual punishment by their captors—to write personal statements acknowledging their past errors in political thought and demonstrating their understanding of the correct (Communist) view. This group method was popularly called "brainwashing."[15] The ideological primary group is not confined to these unhappy instances of twentieth-century totalitarianism but is evinced in such eminently respectable (at least in retrospect) religious groups as medieval Franciscans, Reformation Dissenters, or even apostolic Christianity itself.

Though they differ in the respects just noted, these three varieties of group still deserve the appellation "primary." In all of them the ties that bind are strongly affective, intimate, and "organic," and enjoin a broadly interpreted mutual responsibility or relatively unconditional loyalty to the particular others who make up the group.

These distinctions between the types of primary group bonds clarify the question of primary groups and totalitarianism in the modern world. The thesis that the primary group is withering away under the conditions of modern life is acceptable provided that we interpret "primary" in the first sense suggested above, as the primordial primary group. Personal primary groups, on the other hand, are still very much with us and show no signs of dying out (at least short of the circumstances described by George Orwell in *1984*). Indeed, the contemporary middle-class American family may be said to be joining the ranks of the personal primary group. Traditionally built along stricter patriarchal lines, the family in America and in other countries has been moving away from the primordial group form toward the personal group form. This process is suggested by the title of a sociology text: *The Family, From Institution to Companionship.*[16]

The second thesis, that the absence of primary groups facilitates tyranny, is more difficult to assess. The existence of primordial groups unquestionably imposes barriers to the ultimate penetration of the state into the personal lives of individuals, but does little to prevent the establishment of political autocracy: witness the peasant empires of India and China as well as of the European Baroque era. In other words, primordial groups inhibit totalitarianism but not authoritarian autocracy.[17] Personal primary groups, being essentially apolitical, have no direct influence on forms of government. There is, however, an indirect relationship to which the proposition under discussion very rightly calls attention. Put most simply, there seems to be, as Nisbet suggests, an inverse relationship between the personal satisfactions individuals receive (in good part through their personal and primordial primary-group attachments) and their proneness to seek gratification through membership in ideological primary groups. Self-immolation on the altar of a cause as an answer to loneliness is a theme expressed in the ancient aphorism "Happy people don't make history."[18]

Finally, the thesis that tyranny opposes primary-group attachments refers to the opposition of totalitarianism to any form of intense affective tie outside the ideological primary group or party cell. As with other aims of totalitarianism, this opposition ultimately runs up against practical social necessities—perhaps the most important in this case being the maintenance of the family unit—but as a tendency or principle of totalitarianism it has great significance. In the form of the ideological group within the party framework, primary ties are very much encouraged by such political régimes.

During the 1960s, roughly the period of the Vietnam War, two social movements occurred in America and spread to other parts of the world as reactions to "anomie." One involved people meeting together in small groups for sensitivity training in an effort to promote personal involvement with others; the other involved people, mostly young and single, living together in small communes.[19] Both movements were part of the new life style that appeared as parts of the counterculture.

Most weekends during this period there were innumerable workshops, encounter groups, and T-groups conducted by more or less reputable organizations and individuals. Business firms sent their executives and employees to various programs, in their own plants as well as at special retreats; college and church groups had programs varying from short demonstrations to training programs lasting several weeks. Those who'd participated in a T-group or who'd undergone sensitivity training saw themselves as part of a new subculture.

At the same time many people sought a refuge from the mass society, the plastic culture, the "death machine," in small communal living groups. Some people moved back to the farm, and others renovated large old houses in the urban slums. Many communal groups were formed as a basis for social change, while most provided a place to withdraw from the larger society. For some groups the experience centered around religion; for others it was supported by drugs. Many communal experiments were short-lived because the members could not "get it together" long enough to provide the organization and facilities for a stable community. But some groups prospered and expanded until they became networks of hundreds of people living in small "family" groups.

This discussion of primary groups in the mass society is intended to serve two purposes. In the first place, it brings out an important role for the sociological analysis of politics by suggesting how a microcosmic social form, the primary group, underlies developments on the macrocosmic political and social levels. In the second place, it may serve to warn us against too-facile explanations of the woes of modern society, explanations which in turn carry their own political implications. Thus, the contention that the loss of "primary-ness" in modern life prepares us all for the tyrant's yoke is often linked to the argument that only a return to (primordial) primary groups can prevent disaster; it follows that a revival of such traditional groupings as the patriarchal family or the "community" is an urgent social necessity. The broader ideological setting for this line of argument is usually a conservatism* that attacks the deracinating and disorganizing effects of the Enlightenment—with its ideals of individualism, reason, and science—in the name of the "community" or of something modestly called "values." This conservative critique of liberal political theory claims to go beyond eighteenth-century simplicities to a more profound understanding of the organic quality of social relationships.

Whether sociological analysis necessarily supports such an ideological position is open to doubt: conservatism perhaps employs too limited a conception of primary attachments and endows them with a valuation that sociology, as such, can neither endorse nor deny. In its challenge to liberal political and social thinking, however, it lifts the question of the functions of group life above the "merely academic" and demonstrates the relevance

---

*To be concerned over the general problem of rootlessness in the mass society, one does not, of course, have to be a conservative.

of sociological analysis for some of the most disquieting problems of our day.

SOCIETIES AS PRIMARY GROUPS

A matter that is pervasive in discussions of primary groups, though one rarely dealt with explicitly, is the question of whether an actual society could be essentially a very large primary group. Such a question obviously bears upon ethical doctrines advocating universal brotherhood.

Primitive or peasant-communal societies are sometimes termed "primary" in order to contrast them with our own individualist and contractual form of social organization. This is reasonably accurate and legitimate, even though it is not very precise. But this is not the same as saying that in these communal societies the permissive, affective, and expressive forms of interpersonal relationship, which we may take to be the core of primary-ness, operate exclusively. It is this latter form of the proposition which is here at issue. Is it possible, then, for members of a society to relate to one another in an exclusively primary fashion?

The answer would appear to be negative. This conclusion involves an argument of social necessity. In order for a society to survive—so this argument runs—it is necessary that certain prerequisites be fulfilled. The prerequisites with which we are here concerned are not biological or physical but have to do with the organization and motivation of human effort in order to get essential tasks performed.

Since people no longer live in the Garden of Eden and since they do not build houses and catch fish by instinct, survival requires the application of skill, discipline, and organization. Furthermore, since such valuable things as power, leisure, food, or a considerate spouse are likely to be scarce, people are more than likely to come into conflict. And if this conflict of interests is not to lead to the "war of all against all" which Thomas Hobbes depicted, there must be some standards, rules, or laws in terms of which conflicts are settled. The burden of enforcing such rules is always left in large part to individual conscience, but there seems little likelihood, considering past experience, that this could ever be the end of the story. Some rules, some of the time, require an enforcing authority, and this authority, be it circuit judge or witch doctor, will have to act objectively and impersonally. An authority cannot simply decide in favor of friends or kinsmen and still perform the adjudicating function. (Any one judge can, of course, but if all judges did so the result would be, literally, anarchy.)*

The necessity for impartial authority and for objective standards of efficiency in task accomplishment means that emotional, affective, or expressive impulses and social bonds—the essence of the primary-group relationship—must inevitably be curbed. Any society that relied exclusively on the rule of spontaneity and warm feeling would find its rabbits uncaught, its fields untended, its sheep untended, its pottery unmade, and its war parties decimated—an excellent way, in short, for a society to make sure that its existence would not be recorded in the annals of history.

But, one might contend, cannot the vital social tasks referred to above be performed *within* the primary group? In primitive societies do not kin groups organize the sheep tending and temple building? The answer is yes, in many cases they do, but this is *in spite of* rather than *because of* their primary character. If we refer to the extended family grouping so common in primitive and not-so-primitive societies as "primary," we are doing so in a loose sense. What we are saying is that, *relative* to the way in which the work of the world gets carried on in our own society, *more* familistic elements are involved in the primitive case. Our society is extreme in the extent to which it plays up *what* individuals can do and plays down *who* they are or what their primary group attachments are, that is, the extent to which it reflects the principles of universalism and achievement rather than particularism and ascription. But the bias of our perspective on other societies should not lead us to conclude that because the formal and objective and universalistic criteria of our own society seem

---

*In this connection we may recall Whyte's remarks about the necessity for "fairness" on the part of the gang leader.

to be relatively minor in some other society, such criteria are absent altogether. They cannot be, and for the reasons suggested above.

Once when Freud was asked for a definition of the capacities of the truly mature individual, he replied, *"Lieben und arbeiten"* —to love and to work. The loving is vital—without it individuals would dry up or blow up. Here the primary group plays its absolutely essential role. But working is also necessary, and for this the primary group, in its primary-ness, is not designed. For such ends individuals organize in terms of different principles.

chapter five

THE INDIVIDUAL AND THE GROUP

INTRODUCTION

So far we have discussed the "external" or sociological focus on societies as made up of groups and the major functions the group performs for the individual, for the organization, and for society itself. The subject matter now becomes more specific and the analysis will deal largely with events that, being laboratory experiments, are by definition of no importance in themselves. The laboratory study attempts to rise above its patent artificiality, however, by virtue of the fact that it is designed to represent more universal tendencies and laws. No one, except possibly the participants themselves, really cares whether Cathy, Al, Sara, Fred, and Ralph form a happy or efficient working group. But the question of whether *five* persons can, under certain conditions, reach agreement faster than *four* persons—that might be intriguing. In terms of the immediate group, the outcome of its deliberations is likely to be totally inconsequential; theoretically speaking, however, it may confirm or suggest some significant hypotheses. In the long run, too, the results may have very practical application.

In the previous chapter considerable use was made of the distinction between primary and secondary groups. Not only did this distinction help to clarify various situations but there was a reverse effect as well, and the situations discussed helped to clarify the meaning of these concepts. Thus it is useful to think of primary and secondary not simply as two types of groups but as labels for contrasting forms of social relationship; groups, that is, may conveniently be characterized as having a predominance of one or the other form. This may at first glance seem like a quibble over definitions, but terms often reflect rather different conceptions—some narrower and some broader, some sterile and some fruitful—of what one is observing.

It is more helpful to use primary and secondary (or "expressive" and "instrumental") in the sense of forms of social relationship because in this way the terms become more generalizable and therefore more applicable to other fields and to other levels of social organization. They lead us to ask questions about how we are to recognize primary or expressive behavior or about how primary-expressive behavior fits in with secondary-instrumental behavior in the fabric of interpersonal communication. In effect, our attention is shifted by this broader yet more precise usage from the level of social groups to the level of social behavior, from people's memberships to people's interaction, from an external consideration of the group as a unit to internal consideration of what makes groups tick. We are prodded into looking at internal group structure and group process and into asking questions about what particular acts mean, how they affect an individual's position in the group, and how the group develops over a period of time. The chapters that follow, then, will shift from the more macroscopic to the more microscopic level and turn to a field of study which for the most part has been opened up since 1950.

This field is usually referred to as "small-group analysis" or "group dynamics," and it has mostly been dominated by social psychologists. This gives it a very heavy experimentalist hue, which in turn means that there is more concern with problems of method than we have previously encountered and correspondingly less concern with placing a given piece of research in the total picture. Whatever "total picture" is presented in the experimentalist's report is usually contrived to fit the particular series of experiments carried on. The result is that fragmentation of the field to which reference was made in the first chapter. To organize this diversity into a relatively coherent picture requires a certain amount of grouping, omitting, and equating; this has its dangers, but the risk—to adopt the cliché—is a calculated one.

This chapter, and the two that follow, are built around the following three questions:

What is the effect of the group on the individual?

What is the nature and function of group culture?

What are the patterns of relations among group members?

Each of these questions, when pursued far enough, leads into the others, and investigators themselves have frequently crossed the boundaries in pursuit of the answers. Nonetheless, the questions may serve as the starting points for discussion.

WHAT IS THE EFFECT OF THE GROUP ON THE INDIVIDUAL?

The discussion of this question may be begun by distinguishing between that research which has emphasized instrumental activity and that research which has emphasized expressive activity. The former is exemplified by the study of group influences on the individual's thinking and perception; the latter, by the study of group influence on the individual's emotional life.

Instrumental Emphasis

In recent years a considerable amount of experimentation has been devoted to the question: to what extent and under what conditions is the individual's ability to perform tasks and to perceive stimuli encouraged, inhibited, or molded by the social influences deriving from the group?

Effect of the Group on the Individual's Motivation. In the early 1900s social psychology was much interested in comparing the performance of individuals when they were alone and when they were "together." Being "together" can mean before a passive audience, with coworkers, or with competitors, but it does not include actual cooperative effort where the group works and interacts as a group. Most of these studies showed that the individual was more likely to be positively stimulated when in the company of others than when alone. The most general name for this is, to use the psychologist Floyd Allport's term, "social facilitation"—a diffuse excitability and hyperactivity. This stimulation results in a greater quantity (or an increased speed) of work, along with a tendency to a greater number of errors (or a lower quality of product). Individuals given verbal-association tests before audiences tend to be more inhibited and less free-ranging in their answers than when tested by themselves. (This is not to say that when individuals *interact* in a group they necessarily show less imagination; actually the tendency is for the mutual stimulation to encourage responses the individual would not have made by himself. This will be discussed further below.) Individuals working for some time in front of or alongside others show greater variation in output than when alone, but after a while this effect, as well as the others noted above, wears off. All this suggests that the stimulus provided by the presence of others has sometimes and in some ways (with respect to speed or quantity) an encouraging effect and at other times and in other ways (with respect to quality) an inhibiting effect.[1]

More abstractly, perhaps the most significant generalization that can be made from this tradition of research on individuals, alone and with others, is that behavior depends on the nature of the task and on the nature of the individual's perception of her or his relation to the group. Since the tasks assigned to the subjects in these laboratory experiments were of a fairly mechanical nature, the conclusions are necessarily of a very limited order: we know something about the conditions under which arithmetic problems are done most speedily or most accurately, but this is not very important information. On the other hand, the recognition that the individual's perception of the social environment influences behavior, that reacting *with* is actually a reacting *to*, is much more suggestive. It moves us beyond the conception of general excitability, akin to the phenomenon observable in milling cattle, to the awareness that overt behavior may differ from internal stimulation. The presence of others may not "facilitate" but may rather depress the level of output of the individual, as any shy student can testify.[2] Or, on a more complex level, individuals may form, or perceive themselves to be, a group which takes some pleasure in resisting the efforts of the experimenter. This would be comparable to the restriction of output practiced in the Bank Wiring Observation Room. Thus while it may be true that the presence of others has an arousing effect on the individual (and if the "others" were of the opposite sex the effect would presumably be even greater), the way in which the individual behaves does not usually reflect this stimulation in any very direct way. The individual has in the course of life already acquired too many ways of interpreting and reacting (the individual's "personality structure"), and groups are too different in their organization and tone to permit us to set forth any simple laws about how "groups" affect "individuals."

One reason for the mixed results in the early together and apart experiments is suggested by more recent research that indicates that the presence of others during a learning experiment has a facilitative effect on the dominant (most likely) response, hindering learning when the dominant response is incorrect and helping learning when the dominant response is correct. For example, in an experiment with forty-five male and thirty-nine female undergraduates, each subject followed a maze with a stylus either alone or in the presence of others. For one maze, the subject had only two choices each time there was a branch in the maze, so the chance of finding the correct solution was 50 percent or higher. That is, the dominant (most likely) response would be correct most of the time. For the other maze, the subject had to choose between four alternatives at each branching point, so the dominant response was incorrect and the subject could be right only 25 percent of the time. Under these conditions the subjects who were coactors made fewer errors than those working alone on the maze where dominant responses were likely to be correct. On the maze where dominant responses were likely to be incorrect, subjects performing alone made fewer errors than those coacting. In other words, being aroused by the presence of others only helps when it helps to be aroused.[3]

Effect of the Group in Changing Individual Attitudes and Behavior. Suppose a group of people decides, as a group, to make some change in behavior or attitudes—for example, to work more or to eat less. How committed is the individual to this decision? Research on this question has given rise to three interrelated generalizations: that group change is easier to bring about than is change of individuals separately; that its effects are more permanent; and that it is more likely to be accepted if the individual participates in the decision. Let us look briefly at each of these.

The psychologist Kurt Lewin states the first generalization as follows: " . . . it is usually easier to change individuals formed into a group than to change any one of them separately."[4] Based on his experience in getting people to eat unusual foods during wartime, to increase productivity, to become less prejudiced, and so on, Lewin's proposition makes the assumptions that people like to live up to group norms and that they are susceptible to appeals coming from outside the group. The first assumption is a familiar one and appears to be widely acceptable, but the second cannot be taken for granted. That is to say, by a powerful extragroup appeal, such as to patriotism, one may swing the group from a position successfully defined as unpatriotic to one defined as patriotic. Unless this sort of leverage is available, however, it may not be at all easy to make a group change. Indeed, it would be simpler to reconstitute the group or work on individual opinion leaders. Thus attitude changes in a group context may or may not be easier to bring about than changes outside of that context, depending on various conditions which research has yet to clarify. Lewin's proposition has become something of a slogan among "group relations" workers—perhaps because they tend to assume that *their* morality is unquestionably superior to the morality of those whom they seek to change—but it lacks the preciseness desirable in scientific generalizations.

The supposed greater permanence or effectiveness of an attitude change that takes place in the group context stems also from the individual's assumed desire to live up to group norms. It

63

follows that the stronger the group bonds, the more deeply anchored the individual's attitudes. It also follows that where the "group" being changed is merely an aggregate (for example, a temporary coming-together of students or workers), no such effects can be expected; if changes do occur they cannot be ascribed to any truly group effect. Aggregates of this sort have sometimes been used in research, to demonstrate putative truths about *group* behavior, but this is a logical error even though it is reasonable to apply the generalization about greater permanence to both aggregates and groups.

That the generalization might not be valid is suggested by the fact that what the group grants, the group can take away: it may decide to go along with an admonition to eat whole-wheat instead of white bread, but it may later decide to go back to its former habits. The group context, then, is like extra weight—it makes for momentum as well as for inertia. And in the social world, as in the physical world, bodies do not continue forever on the same path without being subject to contrary forces. What this implies for would-be changers of groups is that they cannot simply induce the desired change and then lean back and rely on any "laws of permanence of group change," for under new external pressures the whole group may shift back again just as completely and "permanently" as it did for the original group reformer. Unlike the individual context, furthermore, the group context involves internal sources of change in the factionalism that is likely to characterize any group. All of which is not to deny that a group change is "likely" to be "more" permanent than an individual change, but the words in quotation marks should serve as reminders of the precariousness of these generalizations.

The proposition that group decisions are more likely to be effective if the individual participates in their making can in good part be equated with the rule that group discussion is more effective than exhortation. Very often this is so, but research indicates that it need not necessarily be so, and that even when the rule *does* hold, we are not sure just why it does.

A review of the literature on group decision comes to a similar conclusion, worth quoting as an illustration of the fact that we often do not know *why* something happens, and that every piece of research is likely to raise two new questions before it settles one old one. The authors find the principal shortcoming of the research in its failure to eliminate alternative and conflicting explanations of the same phenomenon.

> A beginning has hardly been made at exploring the basic factors underlying this relation between participation procedure and goal acceptance, or the exact conditions under which this relation holds. One possibility is that a participation procedure increases the likelihood that a goal will be set which is congruent with individual goals. That this is not the whole story, however, is indicated by the fact that initial preferences are sometimes set aside in favor of the group goal. Another possibility is that because of the discussion involved in setting the goal members are more likely to have adequate knowledge of the goal and of its value to themselves and to the group, as well as a realistic view of its attainability. A somewhat different explanation would be that a positive evaluation of the goal is derived from hearing that other group members value it. Thus if the goal is definitely desired by some members and this becomes apparent through the discussion, their associates may either change their judgments of the goal or work toward it simply as a means of helping their friends. On the other hand, when the goal is imposed from without or by group leaders, resistance or apathy may be attributable to the fact that no member gets a chance to communicate his preference for it. Over and above any tendency to resist being told what to do, which is probably quite general, there may well be a hesitancy to change in any way that might be felt to violate the expectations of one's associates. These suggested explanations for the effectiveness of group decision do not begin to exhaust the possibilities. Determining the specific mechanisms underlying this phenomenon is an important research problem for the future.[5]

Thus, despite the research done on the effect of a group decision in changing individual attitudes, very few firm conclusions have emerged. This is not a total failure, however, since the research has succeeded to a considerable extent in clarifying the questions to be asked.

Effect of the Group on the Individual's Perception.   Further insight into how the individual's opinions, and even perceptions, can come to reflect those of the group are provided by experiments performed by the social psychologists Muzafer Sherif and Solomon Asch.

Some years ago Sherif began to experiment with individual and group reactions to the "autokinetic effect." This is a name for the fact that in a darkened room where there are no visible perceptual standards which can be used for orientation, a person will invariably perceive a fixed point of light as a moving one— the light will appear to move back and forth slightly, though in fact it does not. Peering into a boxlike arrangement in which nothing could be seen save for the apparently wavering point of light, Sherif's subjects were exposed to what psychologists refer to as an ambiguous stimulus situation. After each of a series of observations through the experimental peephole, subjects reported how much the light seemed to move. Each individual's reports came to center about a norm: two inches for one subject, three for another, and so on. Then the subjects were put into groups of twos and threes and again asked to give their estimates of movement, but this time in the presence of fellow subjects. From this confrontation with dissenting views emerged a new, group norm different from the previous norms of the separate individuals. The group members did not consult one another in order to agree on the group norm: they simply continued to give their own estimates and to hear the estimates of others. They converged toward a norm through a series of mutual modifications which, according to the subjects' later reports, were not consciously intended.

Once the shared group norm had been established, the groups were broken up and the individual subjects were again asked to record their judgments in private. It was found that the individuals maintained the group norm under the new circumstances, thus carrying with them, in their perceptual apparatus, the definition of "reality" that had been unconsciously implanted by the group.[6]

A series of experiments by Asch followed a similar procedure, with certain important variations. The groups were larger, consisting of seven or eight members; the stimulus was made unambiguous, subjects being asked to compare and to match lines of various lengths; and the experimenter had arranged for all but one of the subjects to be stooges. They would purposely and unanimously give a wrong answer and so expose the one "naive" subject to a conflict between the subject's senses and his or her desire to join the majority. Asch's question was then, would the naive subjects be rebels or would they yield to group pressures?

It turned out that approximately one-quarter of the fifty naive subjects never wavered from the true path throughout their series of eighteen trial estimates. Approximately one-third of the subjects went with the majority and against the clear evidence of their senses for over half the time. The other subjects fell between these two extremes. Those who yielded did not all do so in the same way or for the same reasons. Asch describes three types of yielding:

> (1) *Distortion of perception* under the stress of group pressure. In this category belong a very few subjects who yield completely, but are unaware that their estimates have been displaced or distorted by the majority. These subjects report that they came to perceive the majority estimates as correct.

> (2) *Distortion of judgment.* Most submitting subjects belong to this category. The factor of greatest importance in this group is a decision the subjects reach that their perceptions are inaccurate and that those of the majority are correct. These subjects suffer from primary doubt and lack of confidence; on this basis they feel a strong tendency to join the majority.

> (3) *Distortion of action.* The subjects in this group do not suffer a modification of perception nor do they conclude that they are wrong. They yield because of an overmastering need not to appear different from or inferior to others, because of an inability to tolerate the appearance of defectiveness in the eyes of the group. These subjects suppress their observations and voice the majority position with awareness of what they are doing.[7]

Asch subsequently arranged to have a minority of *two* rather than one—either by including two uninstructed subjects in the group or by directing one of the stooges to agree with the naive subject. In both cases the result was the same: a radical reduction in the amount of yielding. On the other hand, the *withdrawal* of the partner after an initial period of agreement with the naive subject reestablished the majority effect in full force. Rather than establishing a habit of independence that persisted, the support-then-withdrawal pattern subjected the naive member to especially intense doubts as to his or her own credibility. Such techniques are not unknown to brainwashers. The amount of yielding decreased somewhat if the majority estimates were outrageously, instead of only slightly, wrong, and the range of the naive subject's errors narrowed somewhat if an instructed subject interposed a "slightly wrong" judgment between the correct and the "very wrong" majority estimate.

Asch also found that the majority effect appeared full strength when the majority consisted of three persons (in a group of four) and that the addition of extra members to the majority did not increase the amount of yielding. When the total situation was reversed and one instructed member who gave the wrong answer was placed in a group of sixteen naive subjects who tended to give right answers, there was no distorting effect. As Asch writes:

> Contagious laughter spread through the group at the droll minority of 1. Of significance is the fact that the members lacked awareness that they drew their strength from the majority, and that their reactions would change radically if they faced the dissenter individually.[8]

An Interpretation of Pressures to Conform.   In the mid-1950s Marie Jahoda outlined a theory of conformity that helps us to understand the results of the Sherif and Asch experiments as well as those of the host of social psychologists who sought to replicate and extend their findings.[9] At the time of Jahoda's research, civil liberties, especially centering on the loyalty oath, were a dominant issue in universities in the United States. Although Jahoda had conducted several surveys about this issue, she does not cite her own research evidence, but rather makes up an incident which she feels illustrates all the processes of conformity which are involved. She notes that any similarity with actual events is purely coincidental.

> A college president together with a faculty committee of four persons considers applicants for a new appointment. The best qualified man is one who is known to be a socialist. Each of the four faculty members initially favors his appointment. The president recommends rejection because of the candidate's unsuitable political views. He adds that such an appointment would furthermore seriously offend a benefactor of the college who is about to make a substantial gift to it. As it happens, in this fictitious example, all four members of the faculty go along with the president's recommendation and reject the candidate.

Since each of the faculty members went along with the president's recommendation, we might suppose that they were all equally conforming. However, Jahoda suggests that we use our imagination to hold confidential conversations with each of them after the event. They turn out to have four different stories:

> Faculty member A says: "I feel awful. I still believe that we should not have considered the candidate's political views. But I couldn't stand up to the President. I admit I acted out of fear. The question of my promotion will come up next week."
>
> Faculty member B says: "We had an interesting meeting. Originally I was quite opposed to the notion of considering a candidate's political views. But I changed my mind. The President made a very good argument against the inappropriateness of socialism for our country. He really convinced me of the mistake of deliberately exposing our students to an unrealistic idealist."
>
> Faculty member C says: "I go to these meetings solely because I have been appointed to the committee. I really am not very much interested in these matters. But it is nice to sit together with the President and my colleagues. It makes me feel good to have close friendly contact with them. And if a group of nice people agree, I am the last to make difficulties. I think we did the right thing today."
>
> Faculty member D says: "This was a really difficult decision

for me. I still believe in academic freedom. But the argument that convinced me was that I know the college depends on getting that gift. After all, you can fight for academic freedom only if you have a college that can pay its expenses. I decided to reject the candidate because the President was right when he said we would never get that gift otherwise."

Jahoda then suggests that these four types can be explained by two underlying dimensions: first, whether the subject was moved by the argument or by pressure, and second, whether his belief was changed or unchanged as a result. This cross-classification is presented in Figure 2.

The process of change by convergence is related to the facts of the case. This is the process by which, for example, the scientist decides to accept or reject a new theory. The process of compliance is based on the power of an authority. In some cases, the authority is represented by the majority opinion of the group. Conformance is based on friendship ties, and consentience on adherence to basic values.

Let us consider what it would take to change the minds of the four faculty members after their meeting with the president. The person who was convinced by the facts should be the easiest to influence. Give this person a set of different facts, and a different decision should be reached. The person who complied through threat of loss of promotion should be a little harder to change. Presumably this person would be free to change only after the promotion were actually given or if in some other way the threat could be removed. More difficult to change would be the person who enjoyed being with a friendly group. Even in another situation, this group might remain a positive reference group and provide an anchorage for opinions. If this person were placed in a new group, the latter would have to appear more salient if the person were to change. Finally, the most difficult to change would be the person who has actually taken over the beliefs of the president. Because the beliefs now belong to the person, it becomes a matter of the person's own integrity to maintain them.

Asch's experiment on judging lengths of lines provides an illustration of the relative strength of these four processes in

	Belief changed	Belief unchanged
Argument	Consentience (Faculty member B)	Convergence (Faculty member D)
Pressure (unrelated to issue)	Conformance (Faculty member C)	Compliance (Faculty member A)

FIGURE 2.   Four Processes of Conformism
Source: Marie Jahoda, "Psychological Issues in Civil Liberties," *American Psychologist* 11 (1956), p. 237. Copyright 1956 by the American Psychological Association. Reprinted by permission of the author and the publisher.

bringing about attitude change or in helping to maintain attitudes once they are formed. Asch showed that individuals could be influenced by a coached majority giving incorrect answers, but that this effect would be countered by having at least one person agree with the subject. Further, the majority would have some influence no matter how extreme its opinion appeared to be. However, over 60 percent of the subjects held out against the majority. Many of these subjects said that they typically held out for their own opinions or that they considered the judgments an individual task. These results illustrate the hypothesis that the process of consentience (in this case defining the task as one of individual judgment) was more powerful than the process of conformance (having a partner). The process of conformance was in turn more powerful than the process of compliance (majority pressure). Finally, the convergence process (modifying the length of the line) was the least powerful.

This brief survey reveals how the experimental investigation of the effect of the group on the individual has moved from simple "social facilitation" to subtle incorporation of group norms. Clearly, this is an advance. But it also behooves us to keep in mind the limits and the inadequacies of what has been done. These limits are of four main varieties.

First, it is evident that these experiments make no claim to have investigated all the possible effects of the group on the individual.

We know from experience that individuals learn all sorts of skills and develop all sorts of feelings from their group environments, and although some research has been carried out in these areas, our knowledge can scarcely be said to be very systematic or exhaustive.

Second, and closely related, is the question of whether the "social norms" studied by Sherif and Asch are representative of social norms in general. This is a perennial problem with all laboratory work and constitutes no special criticism of Sherif or Asch. It is nonetheless important to ask whether behavior observed in the laboratory and that observed in the "real" world are the same in fact or in name only. It would be more a verbal than a scientific achievement to claim that by studying "stopping behavior" at traffic lights one is thereby learning how to stop wars or love affairs.

Third is the danger that "group norms" become an explanation for everything. Further exploration of group behavior can too easily be smothered by the apparently wise but actually trite explanation that this or that happens because of a group norm. This form of legerdemain is comparable to the fondness shown by some anthropologists for explanation in terms of a culture pattern. Why did the Germans support Hitler and the British support Churchill? . . . It was due to the culture patterns of the two nations. Why does one group restrict production and another increase it? . . . Because of the differing group norms. Such statements are acceptable as far as they go, but they do not go very far.

Finally, and most important from the present point of view, the sort of experimentation described above is only in the broadest sense a study of groups at all. These groups—or, more accurately, aggregates of subjects—have very little interaction and almost no organization or structure. The group is merely "the others"—a human backdrop for the individual. There is no reason to believe that the experimenters were unaware of this fact; moreover, it is necessary and desirable that an experimenter attempt to isolate a few variables from the total complexity of things. Nevertheless, we must note that the research discussed so far has only touched the fringes of group behavior and that the techniques described do not seem to be fully capable of handling the central problems of group culture and especially group structure.*

Expressive Emphasis

The effect of the group on the individual is not confined to cognitive and rational mental operations. In addition, there are the influences on the feelings and emotional or expressive life of the individual member. These influences have been studied most directly and explicitly by clinical psychologists and psychiatrists interested in the practice of group psychotherapy.

In group psychotherapy emotionally disturbed individuals meet in groups, rather than individually, with a therapist; the process is something more than simultaneous individual therapy on the one hand and something different from the creation of a primary group on the other. The therapist himself has a central role in the group, but just what that role *should* be—for example, how directive, how friendly, how interpretive—is a matter of dispute among therapists. Max Rosenbaum has described eight of the major "schools" of group therapy that have resulted from these differences of opinion on the role of the therapist, on the relationships between group members, and on the goals of treatment.[11]

1. Group psychotherapy from a psychoanalytic base. This is

*A point of view known as "reference group theory" carries the group-as-backdrop conception to its logical conclusion. Here "the group" refers to all aggregates conceived as having some relevance for the individual's opinions, evaluations, aspirations, and such. Mythical entities such as the Aryan race and statistical categories such as "the rich" are treated as groups along with the sort of interacting bodies referred to as groups in this study. Even when the latter phenomena are denoted, the reference group theorist does not really study groups at all but rather those aspects of the individual's mind that may be seen as involving a group referent. Thus almost any reaction by anybody to anything in terms of some standards associated with any aggregate or category falls within the scope of this theory. The result is not really a *theory* at all but rather a point of view which urges us to recognize that people react in terms of other people and to study this matter more exhaustively.[10]

a group therapy based on the theory and methods of psychoanalysis. The general thrust is to engage in long-term treatment with the goal of achieving major personality change.

2. Existential-experiential approaches. The group leader focuses on the immediate experience. There is much emphasis placed on the individual's despair at *being in the world*. Experiences involving feeling and the goal of *authenticity* are stressed. The group therapist is a very active participant, making full use of his or her personality.

3. Transactional analysis. The group leader emphasizes the *games* that people play, and the *script* of life is analyzed. The group is heterogeneous, with little effort made at diagnostic classification. The unconscious or the root of the patient's problem is not stressed.

4. Gestalt therapy. Group members are encouraged to work with feelings they want to get away from. An effort is made to heighten awareness, with a strong emphasis on the here and now. The leader identifies instances when the group members appear to be playing "games" with each other.

5. Psychodrama. The psychodrama therapist aims for the individual to express feelings with greater ease, and to be spontaneous and creative. To re-create scenes from life that were especially important, the patient acts out experiences from the past or concerns about the future on a stage, with an audience and with the help of "auxiliary egos," persons from the audience who serve as figures in the patient's world. In a typical psychodrama the patient or "protagonist" moves through several scenes. Ideally the patient achieves some catharsis of emotion and some insight into the problem.

6. Group psychotherapy based on humanism and the encounter group. The group leader constantly stresses acceptance and respect for the group member's feelings. Basic growth is believed to be lying dormant in the individual. No attention is paid to diagnostic procedures, since classification is believed to imprison both patient (client) and therapist in preconceived notions as to the client's potential.

7. Behavior therapy. Short-term procedures are used. The therapist is interested in changing specific behavior patterns. The

main techniques used are group desensitization and group self-assertion training. This method is similar to a classroom situation.

8. Supportive and adaptational approaches. These approaches are used mainly in clinics, hospitals, and other institutional settings. There is no effort to achieve personality changes or to resolve deep-seated conflicts. Patients are encouraged to practice new methods of *adaptation*. There is a strong emphasis on homogeneity of patients. Neurotic and psychotic patients are carefully differentiated and placed in different groups. The therapist who leads the group is a definite authority figure, very much the all-knowing doctor. One version of the supportive approach is usually led by a lay person who has dealt successfully with the particular problem involved. This version also uses an inspirational approach that may be similar to a religious conversion. The best-known group of this type is Alcoholics Anonymous, but variations of the method are used by obese persons (Weight Watchers), compulsive gamblers (Gamblers Anonymous), former patients from psychiatric hospitals (Recovery, Inc.), drug takers (Synanon), and Child Abusers Anonymous, among others.

Comparing the various types of therapy groups, one can observe some "curative factors" that are present to some extent in all of them, although factors that are minor or implicit in one approach may be major and explicit in another. These are the aspects of the group process that are associated with an effective cure for the patient. If they occur in the course of the group therapy a cure is more likely. Irvin Yalom has identified ten of these factors or mechanisms: (1) imparting information; (2) instilling hope; (3) universality; (4) altruism; (5) the corrective recapitulation of the primary family group; (6) development of socializing techniques; (7) imitative behaviors; (8) interpersonal learning; (9) group cohesiveness; and (10) catharsis.[12]

In general, therapy groups differ from more ordinary groups in that their aim is individual psychological change (not merely gratification) and their structure is more amorphous and labile. As one psychiatrist with long experience in group therapy has written:

> In therapy groups . . . rigidities and fixed relations and roles must be prevented or the therapeutic process is completely blocked. The group must always remain *mobile*. . . . Each patient must remain a detached entity in whom intrapsychic changes must occur. He cannot give up his autonomous identity . . . but must remain at all times detached and work on his own problems.[13]

Even if this statement is not unconditionally acceptable (one might question, for example, whether the patient must be "at all times" detached), it does suggest something of the unique qualities of the therapy group. These qualities are sources of both strength and weakness: of strength in that they break the molds and habits of the individual's previous interpersonal experience and provide a new social reality from which leverage can be applied to the individual's neurotic tendencies; of weakness or confusion in that the patients, never having experienced such a situation, do not know what is expected of them or how to behave. For a disturbed and insecure individual, to be stripped of his protective roles and definitions-of-the-situation can be a fairly traumatic event.

Group therapy offers an unusual and valuable laboratory situation to the student of small-group behavior. For the patient-member, therapy groups are very much a part of his "real life"; he is deeply involved and participates much more as a total personality (insofar as his emotional difficulties permit) than is the case with the more typical member of the usual experimental group—the college sophomore who is set to work solving puzzles or sending messages. Group psychotherapy has for the most part proceeded by feeling its way along, with the result that there are many schools and rules of thumb but little established theory of group functioning. One can turn this proposition around and say that because there is not enough firm group theory, group therapy has had to operate by trial and error. Whichever the cause and whichever the effect, the result has been that group psychotherapists, when they have tried to be theoretical, have found individual or clinical psychology (particularly, psychoanalysis) so much more capable of dealing with subtle complexities than is small-group theory that they have relied on it almost exclusively as a framework for analysis and as a language for the formulation of hypotheses. This has meant that until recently there was a neglect of specifically social or group variables operating in the therapy situation.[14] In the absence of a systematic concern for group norms and group organization—that is, without theoretical and methodological means for encompassing patterns and styles of group interaction—interpretation is still bound by the clinically derived emphasis on the individual.[15]

The Risky Shift. In the 1960s a rash of experiments were conducted on the phenomenon of the "risky shift." It appeared that individuals who would make conservative decisions about matters involving risk when they were alone would shift to more risky decisions when they took part in a group discussion. Ten years later, after a number of competing theories about the phenomenon had been proposed and tested, the evidence suggested that a number of factors were operating—indeed, all of the factors which operate in any group decision. However, so much research has now been done on this subject that the "risky shift" provides one of the best-documented examples of differences between individual and group problem-solving.

In the late 1950s there was a commonly held belief that group decisions tended to be conservative and mediocre. In contrast, Robert Ziller found that decisions made by group-centered decision-making groups were more risky than decisions made by leader-centered groups.[16] In a later study, James Stoner made a more direct comparison of individual and group decision-making.[17] He found that decisions made by groups were riskier than prediscussion decisions made by individual members of the group. This research served as the starting point for a series of studies designed to determine the generality of this finding and to explain the processes that produced the effect.

Michael Wallach and his colleagues were surprised by the Stoner findings and apparently doubted that the risky-shift phenomenon could be reliably demonstrated.[18] They conducted an experiment with 218 liberal arts university students of both sexes. The students were divided into groups of six, either all males or all females. Before and after group discussion the students were given an opinion questionnaire with twelve hypothetical situations. The central person in each situation could choose between two courses of action, one of which was more risky than the other but also more rewarding if successful. For each situation a subject was asked to indicate the lowest probability of success he or she would accept before recommending that the potentially more rewarding alternative be chosen. The probabilities listed were one, three, five, seven, and nine chances of success in ten, plus a final category (scored as ten) in which the subject could refuse to recommend the risky alternative no matter how high its likelihood of success.

The situations were designed to cover a wide range of content. As examples, three of the situations may be summarized as follows:

1. An electrical engineer may stick with his present job at a modest but adequate salary or may take a new job offering considerably more money but no long-term security.

2. A man with a severe heart ailment must seriously curtail his customary way of life if he does not undergo a delicate medical operation that might cure him completely or prove fatal.

3. A man of moderate means may invest some money he recently inherited in secure blue-chip low-return securities or in more risky securities that offer the possibility of larger gains.

As a result of the group discussions Wallach, Kogan, and Bem found that (1) group decisions exhibit greater risk-taking than appears in prediscussion individual decisions; (2) private decisions after the discussion exhibit the same increased risk-taking; (3) this increase in risk-taking endures over a subsequent period of weeks; (4) no shift in risk-taking level occurs over time in the absence of the discussion process; and (5) the degrees of individual risk-taking and of judged influence within the group are positively related. Subsequent research by others tend to confirm these findings.

Once the phenomenon of the "risky shift" was well documented, the explanation of the behavior was still open. Experimenters sought to account for the shift in different ways. Some varied the facts of the case to be discussed, the responsibility of the members for the decisions; others varied the cohesiveness or the composition of the groups in terms of the basic values of the members; still others noted the implicit demands of the experimenter. All of these factors make a difference.[19]

Facts. Subjects who have more facts or who in general know more about the situation are more likely to take a chance. If they are clear about the relative amount of risk involved in choosing each alternative, they can make a more rational decision. Thus one effect of group discussion is to provide relevant and persuasive arguments that the individual may not have considered before.

Responsibility and Majority Opinion. When subjects feel that the responsibility for the decision has been diffused over the group, the decisions are more risky. In some experiments the risk takers do not appear to be the most persuasive persons in the group, although other research suggests that the risk takers may be more confident of their opinions and have considerable influence, especially when they are in the majority. Since risk takers seem to have been a majority in the population from which most experimental groups are drawn, the shift towards risk tends to reflect the influence of majority opinion, especially when the task is ambiguous.

Social Approval. Subjects will make more risky decisions if they feel that other group members approve of risk-taking, or that the risky choice is more ethical or altruistic. The effect is heightened when group members have strong affiliative motives or are highly interdependent. However, if the group members seem to approve of taking less risk, then the subjects will be more conservative. They will also be more conservative if they are making decisions for another person or group, rather than for themselves.

Group Composition. As in the experiments on social facilitation, some of the group effect in the risky-shift phenomenon may be that the dominant or more likely responses are enhanced as a result of making decisions in the presence of others. But more obvious effects result from the types of personalities composing the group. As in the Asch experiment on conformity, subjects who are high on autonomy are less likely to be influenced by the group. In general, subjects tend to behave in a way that is consistent with their personality characteristics.

Experimenter Demands. Some of the early results of the risky-shift experiments may have been simply a response to the implicit demands of the experimenter, as the situation was defined for the subjects at the beginning of the experiment. In research in which the usual risk-oriented instructions are replaced by more neutral instructions, the risky shift seems to disappear.

CONCLUSION: INDIVIDUAL AND PERSONALITY

This chapter has surveyed the main lines of research on the effect of the group on individual performance. One of the two major shortcomings of this research has already been mentioned: that in the study of the group-individual relationship, the group side of the "equation" has been left largely unspecified; research has, on the whole, neglected matters of internal group organization and process.

But the individual side of the "equation" has perhaps fared no better—and this constitutes the second shortcoming. With the exception of students of psychotherapy, investigators have tended to bypass problems of intrapersonal organization and process. That is to say, the focus has been on the traits of the individual rather than on the dynamics of the personality.

"Individual" is a relatively colorless term referring to the human organism that acts or is the recipient of some influence from outside. "Personality," on the other hand, is surrounded by connotations suggestive of a dynamic entity with an internal structure or system of feeling, thinking, and willing. The former concept can embrace animals or even inanimate objects, but the latter has a specifically human quality and is, in Nietzsche's phrase, "a social structure composed of many souls." If this distinction is acceptable, it follows that to investigate the effects of the group on the *individual* is not too difficult: one puts the individual in a group and then observes whether he or she behaves differently than when alone. But this is not quite the same as studying the effect of group life on the *personality*. That would involve the analysis of a whole complex of influences on an entity capable of reacting in myriad and devious ways. Insofar as the personality is a system, what happens in or to one part is likely to affect other parts by virtue of the rebalancing or re-equilibration which takes place following the original stimulus. We are confronted with a complicated process of assessment on the part of the organism rather than by a simple stimulus-response phenomenon. The process of assessment reflects and is a product of the emotional and cognitive structure which has been built up over a person's lifetime.

In sum, when we deal with the interrelations of group and personality we are taking on a more complicated and difficult task than when we simply deal with the reactions of individuals. The terms employed make little difference, but the broadened conception of the problem certainly does. This conception implies, most importantly, that one has a theory of personality that is both "true" and commensurable with the variable to be used in describing the group context.

This is a very large order, and while it is desirable to see the full scope and all the imponderables of the problem, it is also desirable not to let this awareness become an argument from perfection. We can scarely afford to sit by and await the millennium when we will (somehow) have a fully adequate grasp of all that is involved in social and psychological problems. We have to begin where we are—granted that it is in a state of imperfection—and talk of "the individual" in down-to-earth, simple terms before we can deal with "the personality." But the goal—an understanding of the complex entity called personality in its relation to the group—should never be forgotten. Students of small groups lower their sights at the risk of becoming inconsequential.

chapter six

THE CULTURE OF THE GROUP

This chapter will be concerned with the culture of the group —with the ideas, beliefs, norms, and standards which members of groups hold by virtue of their membership. First, we will note the general significance of the fact that groups possess a "culture." Then we will consider some of the problems involved in studying this phenomenon in a small-group setting.

GROUP PROCESS AND GROUP CULTURE

What takes place when a group tries to solve a problem? A good part of the answer must wait until Chapter 7, which discusses the relations among members—that is, the social structure of the group. In addition to these interpersonal relationships, however, there is that aspect of group process in which ideas and values are brought forth, modified, and extended in the course of group discussion.

At the simplest level, the group creation of ideas and values consists of the process of pooling. Unless the group's members turn out to be absolutely identical in their abilities and outlooks (and this is about as improbable as anything could be), the pooling of their ideas will involve a process different from what would take place were the individuals solving problems by themselves. The *result* of pooling is not necessarily a better product than the individual could turn out, but at this point we are only concerned with distinguishing the constituent parts of this phenomenon called group process. Though pooling is a part of this process, it is usually a minor part—even in the highly mechanical tasks at which laboratory groups typically work. In addition, there are the already noted effects of the group on the individual member: individual thinking and motivation is influenced in such a way that what is available to be pooled is different from what would be available if members wrote out their ideas and mailed them to the experimenter. But social facilitation (or social inhibition, as the case may be), with its effects on the pooling of ideas, scarcely begins to describe, much less to explain, what takes place in group discussion.

The process of group discussion consists in good part of proposals followed by counterproposals, acceptances, modifications, and rejections. New learning takes place, and if Fortune smiles, from inchoate fumblings new ideas and clarifications emerge. This interaction is not devoted exclusively to the problems on the group's official agenda but covers a wide range of topics: how long the session will last, what the group members are going to do afterward, last week's traffic jam, the political doings of the country's leaders, and so forth. From such particulars a sense of solidarity (or its opposite, but we may take the positive alternative for illustrative purposes) is built up among the group's members; a feeling for the limits of relevancy or of good taste or of radicalism emerges. A consensus develops as to what is humorous and what is shrewd. The group begins to deal with new situations in terms of past experiences. It may be a matter of a conscious decision to avoid repeating previous errors or it may be a matter of the unconscious sensitivity to certain stimuli, but in either case the group is proceeding on the basis of a learned response and a tradition. Members may learn not to raise certain sorts of issues because they recognize the group's propensity for sidetracking itself with peripheral concerns; members may learn that to get things done they have to "view with alarm" or "point with pride." As time goes on, more and more little rules and procedures come into being, change, are refined, and are "passed down" to later generations (that is, to next week's session). In sum, all this adds up to a small and incomplete but still recognizable variety of *culture*.

In broad perspective, the amount and kind of culture built up in the ordinary discussion group is negligible. Except in the case of philosophic or literary "circles," the culture of the small group does not appear to add much to the sum total of human achievement. The apparent unimportance, however, is somewhat misleading, for culture, or a set of common meanings, is necessary to the continued operation of any group, primary or otherwise. Cultural meanings are not, of course, created anew for every little group that happens to form, but the tying together, the shaping and refinement of general norms, ideas, and sentiments prevalent in the broader culture is a vital process in small-group development. This is in large part what we mean when we say that people have to learn how to work together.

Each group has a subculture of its own, a selected and modified version of some parts of the larger culture. The significance of these subcultures lies not so much in what they add to the larger culture as in the fact that without its own culture no group would be more than a plurality, a congeries of individuals. The common meanings, the definitions of the situation, the norms of belief and behavior—all these go to make up the culture of the group. With characteristic penetration, Durkheim a half-century ago described this phenomenon and its significance:

> When a certain number of individuals in the midst of a political society are found to have ideas, interests, sentiments, and occupations not shared by the rest of the population, it is inevitable that they will be attracted toward each other under the influence of these likenesses. They will seek each other out, enter into relations, associate, and thus, little by little, a restricted group, having its special characteristics, will be formed in the midst of the general society. But once the group is formed, a moral life appears naturally carrying the mark of the peculiar conditions in which it has developed. For it is impossible for men to live

together, associating in industry, without acquiring a sentiment of the whole formed by their union, without attaching themselves to that whole, preoccupying themselves with its interests, and taking account of it in their conduct. This attachment has in it something surpassing the individual. This subordination of particular interests to the general interest is, indeed, the source of all moral activity.[1]

Culture, then, is a term applicable not only to the large society but to its subgroups as well, and is indeed a fundamental feature of the interaction of human beings.

GROUP PROBLEM-SOLVING

There are two major, and overlapping, approaches to the study of group culture, one being the study of group problem-solving, the other the study of group norms. This section deals with the former, the next section with the latter.

Some studies contrast the problem-solving ability of groups to that of individuals. The results of these studies are relatively meager, especially considering the significance attached to the general problem of the creativity of groups. If individuals associated in groups can under certain conditions surpass themselves and come up with better ideas than they could have managed on their own, then small groups have a new aim and the study of small groups a new urgency. The new aim would be the positive enrichment of human culture, as distinguished from the maintenance of society and the recreation of individuals. The new urgency would arise from the desirability of finding those conditions under which the creative potentials of groups can be maximized. It is perhaps the business world which stands to gain most prominently from learning more about the creative potentials of group problem-solving. The plans and decisions which guide large-scale enterprise in this country are in good part made by committees and conferences. Rightly or wrongly, businessmen and others have come to consider the conference the best means for seeing that the managerial work of this world gets carried on.

In short, billions of dollars rest on the assumption that group decisions are in some sense better than individual decisions.

And what do investigations show? That in many simple tasks, tasks largely of the puzzle or reasoning variety, groups are superior to individuals. Groups give more correct solutions, they have better learning and recall (at least of nonsense words); they make fewer errors and detect them more quickly.[2] Thus in cool, impersonal laboratory problems wherein the checking of logical error is important, groups do better than individuals.

Although the group is usually better at solving problems than the average individual, it is seldom better than the best individual. It is therefore probable that in many cases the apparent superiority of the group results from the presence of *one* superior individual. The group effects in any case should be greater if the groups are composed of subjects who have made high scores as individuals. In terms of time required, groups are more expensive, since the time for a group solution must be multiplied by the number of members in computing the cost of the product. For this reason the group method would seem to require more accuracy, more member satisfaction, or some other positive result in addition to efficiency in terms of units per hour to justify its use.[3]

The difference between individual and group problem-solving derives from two sources. On the one hand, there are the group effects on the ideas available within each individual, to be pooled in the group meeting. These influences—on motivation, perception, and attitudes—were discussed in the previous chapter. On the other hand, the group member is encouraged or constrained in his or her overt contribution by the presence and the attitudes of others. This is a matter partly of group norms and partly of group social structure; these phenomena are discussed in the following section and in Chapter 7, respectively.

In addition to comparing the problem-solving abilities of individuals and groups, it is possible to compare different kinds or conditions of groups with respect to their creative capabilities. Disregarding the native capacities of group members (which would quite clearly affect the quality of the respective group problem solutions), differences between groups reflect the presence of the factors just noted: group norms and group social structure. Where members show a high enthusiasm for group goals—perhaps because they had a hand in setting these goals— they tend to produce more and to be better satisfied with their efforts than where no such enthusiasm exists.[4] Primary and coop- erative group norms have likewise been shown to affect group product, though not necessarily by increasing its amount or quality (see below). Structural variables, such as size or leader- ship, also help to determine the problem-solving ability of a group (see Chapter 7).

With respect to all these variables, research has revealed no unambiguous rules for constructing creative groups. Nor has it clearly demonstrated the conditions under which individuals rather than groups produce better solutions to problems. Execu- tives responsible for establishing the methods of decision-making and problem-solving for their organizations may be able to ac- quire insights and wisdom from small-group research, but as yet there is a dearth of applicable and at the same time adequately grounded and reliable findings.

Perhaps because of this very dearth, one method of group problem-solving has created quite a stir in some business and even in a few governmental circles. This is the technique known on Madison Avenue as "brainstorming," which attempts to maxi- mize the flow of ideas in a group by eliminating any critical or even realistic impulses a member might have. These critical and appraisive functions are postponed by the group leader, who rules "out of order" any member who begins to indulge in "nega- tive thinking." Thus presumably one eliminates major restraints on creativity.

Unfortunately for the promoters of brainstorming, individuals are usually found to produce more ideas per person when work- ing alone. Some of the apparent superiority of brainstorming groups may have resulted from the fact that superior individuals were recruited to take part, since "supergroups" composed of high-performing individuals do better than those composed of individuals who are low performers.[5]

Brainstorming makes at least two assumptions which are open to question. It assumes, first, that people think most creatively when there are no obstacles to the stream of consciousness; and second, that among the torrent of ideas (actually, associations) there are bound to be some good ones. The first of these assumptions is a version of the "an artist is like unto a little child" theory of creativity: solving problems is a matter of letting natural inclinations run free. The second assumption reflects the fondness of Americans for identifying quantity with quality.

Observations of different types of group problem-solving suggest that group decision behavior combines individual decision processes with a conflict-resolving process when members do not agree. Some of the variations of decision rules for resolving conflicts between individuals include the proposition that "truth wins" no matter how many persons in the group discover the truth, majority rule, and consensus (where members discuss their differences until a new solution can be found to which all can agree). The various methods of group decision-making can be compared with respect to the criterion for an acceptable decision, the number of steps in the decision-making process, the opportunities for a combination of two or more minorities in opposition to a leading candidate or proposal, or other criteria.[6]

In the typical laboratory experiment with initially leaderless groups of persons who are equal in status, explicit decision rules are not usually proposed. However, all groups tend to have implicit rules that govern the decision-making process. Most groups of university students appear to use an equalitarian process in which each strategy advocated by a member during a discussion has an equal probability of being selected. Group members try to be fair to each member so that as a result of a group decision most members of the group can come close to realizing their own individual levels of aspiration. As a result, the group decision is often simply the median of the individual decisions.

GROUP NORMS

An important means of conceptualizing a group's culture is in terms of its norms. We have already seen in the studies by Asch how group norms influence individual perceptions and judgments, and in the Western Electric researches how norms guide individual behavior and so affect group output. Norms help to identify and to define the group; they thereby help to establish the status of the individual in the larger society. They provide meaning, or a definition of the situation, and so help the individual to understand or come to terms with an ambiguous reality. Sherif's experiments illustrate this function of group norms. Moreover, acceptance of group norms by the member is a helpful—possibly even a necessary—procedure for furthering the goals of the group or of the individual. Acceptance promotes *group* goals because it facilitates the establishment of working procedures and the coordination and disciplining of individual contributions; it promotes *individual* goals (assuming these are distinct from those of the group) because it makes allies, or at least neutrals, of one's companions. Finally, group norms are shared by members because of the potential sanctions the group can invoke in the case of deviants. The application of "group pressure" can take a wide variety of forms, from the relatively subtle and implicit ones seen in Asch's experiments to the overt violence described by Thrasher in his study of gangs.

Thus group norms are shared because of the potential gratifications involved in doing so and the potential deprivations involved in not doing so. How "deep" group norms go is another question: a member may accept them wholeheartedly, convinced of their essential justice and truth, or he may accept them under protest, conforming for the sake of his own or the group's advancement. Just where any given individual stands with respect to any specific norm or value is not easily determined—not only because laboratory methods have difficulty in assessing the individual's "true" feelings, but also because the individual himself may not know precisely how much he believes and how much he conforms. Asch's experiments suggest some of this indeterminateness on the part of the individual subjected to group pressure on his perceptual norms. The adoption by concentration-camp inmates of the values of their oppressors, an acceptance which is much more than mere conformity under duress, is dramatic evidence of the power of coercion to compel conversion.[7]

Requirements for the Analysis of Group Norms

Of particular significance for the field of small-group research are those studies which (a) employ some new technique for measuring group norms, (b) attempt to survey and catalogue group norms according to some systematic theory of cultural variations, or (c) show in a reasonably precise way how a given norm is causally related to some other aspect of group process, such as the group product or the group social structure or the attitudes of the individual members.

The most famous study meeting these criteria has already been described: Lippitt and White's study of authoritarian, laissez-faire, and democratic group atmospheres. Though this research is often referred to as a study of leadership or of "social climate," it is equally a study of cultural norms as these guide the behavior of a key person in the group, the adult counselor. Lippitt and White did not try to manipulate group atmosphere or group culture directly—that is, they did not attempt to instill or arrange *group* norms. Instead, they manipulated the group leader and hoped that his behavior would have a decisive influence on the group as a whole. This expectation turned out to be well-founded—the resulting group behaviors varied in accordance with the norms of leadership.

It is one thing to study a group and to find that its members share norms—that they are passionately for or against some popular singer, for example, or that they look down on the workers in the next office—and it is something else to analyze experimentally the effects of those norms that you have good reason to believe are of some importance in the society at large. The former sort of investigation can never fail to come up with some list of norms. But since the existence of norms is an old story, little is added to social science when it is revealed that Girl Scouts and octogenarians have their beliefs and standards just as do Western Electric workers. Granted that it is more desirable to have a systematic classification of group norms than ad hoc description of norms as they happen to be found in this or that group, on what basis should the classification be made? While the range of potential classifications is almost unlimited, it seems likely that individuals' attitudes toward the group process itself—that is, their conception of desirable human relations—will be of particular pertinence.

Some Examples of the Study of Norms

Cooperation and Competition. One study dealing with widely recognized types of norms compared groups in which *cooperation* was made a dominant value with groups in which *competition* was encouraged. In this experiment, five-man groups of college students were set to work on puzzles and human-relations problems. In some groups individuals were rewarded in terms of the success of the group as a whole; in other groups (the competitive ones) they were rewarded for their individual contributions. The conclusions of this study were as follows:

> The interdependent relationship in which cooperation is rewarded seems to lead to strong motivation to complete the common task and to the development of considerable friendliness among the members. The problem-solving process is characterized by specialization of effort along with the effective coordination of the separate activities.... Finally, this type of relationship [cooperative] is characterized by a highly effective communication process which tends to promote maximal publication of ideas and great mutual influence .... There was no clear difference between the two types of groups in terms of the amount of individual learning which occurred during the discussions, but with respect to group productivity the cooperative groups were clearly superior.[8]

The superiority of cooperation over competition in this experiment probably owes a good deal to the difficulty of forcing small groups of fellow students, meeting face to face, into open competition with one another[9] as well as to the known advantages of pooling ideas—which the cooperative conditions favored. It seems doubtful that the study has broader relevance for social and economic relationships.

Primary- and Secondary-Group Norms. Another study, carried out by Olmsted, attempted to compare the effects on group structure and group process of another pair of norms that have a recognized place in sociological thinking. This study contrasted four-man groups having primary norms with groups in which secondary standards were operative. The norms, rather than being indigenous to the group, were experimentally induced in both cases. The implantation was done by telling each newly formed group before it began its discussion session that "science" had determined the best way to run a group discussion: in twelve groups this "scientific" advice pointed up the values of primary relationships—warm, solidary, person-oriented, and so forth—while in twelve other groups "science" was said to support secondary values—cool, practical, impersonal, businesslike attitudes. (After the experimental session had been concluded, it may be added, the members were disabused of the specious notion that science was yet in a position to speak authoritatively on the subject.)

The two types of norms tended to bring into being different forms of social organization—that is, different patterns of interaction and different systems of role differentiation. The primary type of group showed a greater degree of differentiation among members in status, amount of participation, and estimated contribution to the solution of group problems. The secondary type of group tended to be more argumentative and more competitive; members showed more instability in their positions in the group and gave evidence of the sort of "status anxiety" that has been found to characterize competitive groups in other contexts.[10] The members of the primary type of group were more in agreement as to who was performing leadership functions and were also more content with their greater degree of hierarchy and differentiation than were the members of the secondary type with their greater equality. In their development of, and respect for, a hierarchical differentiation of roles, the primary type of group in some respects resembles the communal or organic society while the secondary type is more similar to the competitive, contractual, and individualist society. Thus this study suggests that the same conceptual tools are useful for the analysis of both small-scale and large-scale social systems.[11]

CONCLUSION

Perhaps the most notable characteristic of experimental studies of the types of norms we have been discussing here is their paucity. Although there are more experimental studies of the influence of group standards on individual judgments than on any other subject in social psychology, and although there have been a rash of studies of competition in two-person games, there simply have not been many studies that have attempted to experiment with norms of the sort found in larger societies.

More broadly, that aspect of group life which has here been called "culture" has not been widely recognized as deserving of special attention. Particular problems involving cultural elements have been frequently investigated—for example, in studies of suggestibility or of communication—but these, like the general acknowledgment that "culture is very important," do not fulfill our obligations. We have, in small-group research, the opportunity for tracing the operation, the creation and dissipation, of ideas and values within a definable context. To take advantage of this opportunity we need more careful definitions of the phenomena in question and of the particular variables and analytic categories with which we hope to encompass the problem. We need a systematic and comprehensive appraisal of what we think we know and can reasonably expect to discover. We need to be at once more general and more subtle, more bold and yet more modest. In short, we need better theory.

chapter seven

THE SOCIAL STRUCTURE OF THE GROUP

The phenomenon that the student of the small group observes typically consists of organisms making noises at one another. To make sense of this phenomenon, the observer must make distinctions; by introducing clarifying conceptions he or she tries to bring order into a buzzing confusion. In this study, the subject matter is conceived of as consisting of individual personalities sharing common ideas and values and forming structured relationships—that is, in terms of the abstractions of personality, culture, and social structure. These are three different kinds of abstraction from the same concrete objects and events. We have so far considered the first two of these. We now turn to the third way of abstracting—namely, in terms of social structure.

Social structure may be thought of as the patterns of relations among members of a society or of a group. In the small group, this is largely a matter of role differentiation and integration with respect to both instrumental and expressive activity. In an investigation of behavior in groups, the observer invariably "confronts" both culture and social structure. Except among animals (most notably among the social insects, such as bees and ants), who may be said to possess a social structure without a culture, the distinction between the two is analytical, not concrete: they are not separate entities but differing aspects of the same reality: we do not see culture in one corner and social structure in another. Despite this dual nature of group life, however, it is possible to emphasize one abstraction or the other: the investigator may concentrate on the quality of ideas brought forth in a group (without caring how group members relate to one another), or may focus upon relationships of dominance and submission in the group (neglecting the beliefs and values of the several members).

In this chapter we are concerned with the latter emphasis. Cultural variables play differing roles in the alternative approaches to group social structure considered here—in some instances they are largely neglected. In all our cases, however, what is central is the organization and interrelations of people.

This chapter emphasizes differences among approaches more than similarities. It is, moreover, selective: major approaches are discussed at some length, but no attempt is made to find room for all available research.[1] Though every approach likes to claim generality, the division into "special perspectives" and "general theories" seems both reasonable and convenient. Within the former category, the now-familiar distinction between affective and instrumental emphases provides the principle of organization.

SPECIAL PERSPECTIVES

The Group as a Network of Affective Relations

Sociometry. In dealing with affective relations within the group, the technique of study that has probably gained more currency than any other is known as sociometry. It should be noted that the term has both a special and a general meaning.

Sociometry in its *special* sense is associated directly with the psychiatrist J. L. Moreno. Moreno saw affective bonds, and the propensity to form them, as the crucial human and social fact. Around this fact, and with the aim of promoting that spontaneity and creativity of action that he saw as the *summum bonum* of human experience, Moreno built a broad—nay, cosmic—theory of man, society, and destiny. In connection with but separable from this theory, Moreno developed several techniques for studying group relations. One of these, largely therapeutic in its intention, is psychodrama, wherein the therapist involves the group members in role-playing situations and so encourages them to act out their inner psychological problems. Under a psychodrama director's enthusiastic stimulation, unusual and intense group situations that provide excellent material for the student of group behavior are created. But from the point of view of an observer (as distinguished from a participant), the material presented is only as useful as his conceptual tools permit: he only sees what he sees.

Another technique developed by Moreno is the sociometric test. Group members are given questionnaires asking whom they like and dislike, or more specifically, whom they would like to eat with, work with, live with, sit next to, and so on. These provide a picture of the group's internal structure, its cliques, loyalties, and leadership. (See the example of Newcomb's groups in Chapter 3.) In somewhat looser forms than Moreno himself prescribed, such tests have been very widely used by social psychologists and others who do not necessarily share Moreno's theoretical constructions; hence the more general sense in which the term sociometry is used. In this sense, sociometry consists of any device which asks group members how they feel about each other. In a further refinement and elaboration ("relational analysis"), members are asked not only what they think of others but what they think others feel about them.[2]

Sociometric techniques are useful practically in making up work or play groups, classroom seating arrangements, and the like so that they will function more effectively. They are useful theoretically in providing insights into group structure as it is perceived by its inhabitants. The insight of perhaps the broadest significance from the viewpoint of this study is the discovery that within the average small (and even primary) group it is possible to distinguish a "psychegroup" and a "sociogroup."[3] The former is more personal, spontaneous, and effective (that is, it exhibits most clearly those qualities we have previously ascribed to the primary group), while the latter grouping is more cool, more formal and impersonal (that is, it possesses secondary qualities). Psychegroup and sociogroup do not represent factions or cliques, but rather are two different structures into which the group aligns itself depending on the occasion. Operationally speaking, the psychegroup is defined in terms of the choices made by group members (and the resulting pattern deriving from these choices) of those with whom they would like to *relax;* the sociogroup is defined by choices of those with whom they would like to *work.* Thus Charlie, a good guy, might be the center of the group in its psychegroup manifestation, while June, the hard worker, would provide the nucleus of leadership in the group's sociogroup character. All this, of course, follows from the fact that people discriminate among others not only in terms of *whether* they are attracted or repelled by them but in terms of *what* they like or dislike about them.

Because of their usefulness and their relative simplicity, sociometric techniques are employed today in almost all studies of group functioning, very often in accompaniment with whatever other techniques particularly interest an investigator. Thus from a rather special beginning sociometry has evolved into a widely employed tool for small-group study.

It is therefore especially necessary to keep certain limitations in mind. In the first place, as Shils has noted, sociometry "does not record actual association; it does not describe actions; it does not provide a picture of the actually existing group relations and group tensions in a concrete situation. . . ."[4] It records only what people say (write) and has the virtues and limitations of any such subjective data.

Second, sociometry imposes strict limits on the kind of response the subject is permitted to make. The subject must be either pro or con, attracted or repelled. If the subject is ambivalent, as people are wont to be, there is no way of making this known except by not choosing. This restriction is wonderfully convenient from the point of view of the investigator but leaves much to be desired as a method of apprehending the complexities of reality.

Third, and this is closely related to the previous criticism, the data obtained are *conscious* opinions presented to an outsider. If a group member does not wish to admit certain feelings (especially of hostility) either to himself or to another, the sociometric data may be distorted. To be sure, these same objections can be made about almost any form of questionnaire and they thus constitute one of the burdens of social science generally, but the likelihood of distortion would appear to be increased by the bald simplicity of the sociometric questions.

Finally, sociometry—at least its purer form which concerns itself with attractions and repulsions after the manner of a latter-day social physics—tends to assume that pro and con feelings constitute *the* structure of the group. Instead of being taken as one kind of datum about group structure, the sociometric diagram has often been accepted as portraying the essence of group life. For example, a generation of sociometrists assumed that leadership is simply a question of sociometric popularity.[5]

Sociometric attention to *affective relationships* has resulted in neglect of instrumental or *task-oriented activity*. Since it is the interrelation of these two types of behavior that is fundamental to group life, this specialization of attention involves more than merely a question of the division of labor among investigators. This one-sidedness is especially deplorable given the rudimentary conception of psychological forces with which sociometry typically operates.

Psychoanalysis. In Chapter 5 the point was made that psychoanalysis has been concerned with the affective side of the personality as it operated in the group psychotherapeutic context. It was also stated that group psychotherapists had tended to think in terms of aggregates of individual cases when considering group therapy and to employ the intellectual constructs derived from therapy with individuals rather than more truly sociological theories about emergent group properties. These propositions, while valid in general, admit of some exceptions, and in the present context of the affective relations within groups, these exceptions are worth noting briefly.

In 1921 Freud published his *Group Psychology and the Analysis of the Ego*. Its basic point is that groups are held together by a common identification with a leader. Freud puts it this way: "A primary group ... is a number of individuals who have substituted one and the same object for their ego ideal and have consequently identified themselves with one another in their ego."[6] To Freud, the solidarity of groups is rather more problematic and uncertain than it is likely to seem to us. Freud is generally very much impressed with the anarchic, "narcissistic," and centrifugal character of man and society, and consequently group life is not (to redirect a phrase from Adam Smith) "a simple and obvious system of natural liberty," but a rather odd circumstance that calls for explanation. The explanation Freud gives is pretty much in line with the general tendency of his thought: on the one hand there is an unlikely (and fortunately irrelevant) conjecture about the first human groups, back before the dawn of history, and on the other hand there is the dramatic conception of the transformation of psychic impulses. Though *Group Psychology and the Analysis of the Ego* scarcely represents one of Freud's more trenchant and elaborate analyses, it does evince his characteristic insight into the crucial significance of the fact that emotional attachments of various kinds can be converted into other kinds of attachments or can be repressed or rechanneled, and furthermore, that without such transformations human association would be all but impossible. Freud's emphasis on affective ties with the leader is scarcely an adequate theory of social structure, but it does have the virtue of recognizing that devotion to a leader is *one* way of overcoming the centrifugal forces of group life.

The interest in this country in children's problems of classroom adjustment, and the social worker's practice of "group work" with disadvantaged youngsters, have stimulated further thinking along the lines laid down by Freud. One of the most fruitful contributions has been made by the psychologist Fritz Redl.

In an article on "Group Emotion and Leadership,"[7] Redl concerns himself with the "constituent group emotions" that are "basic to the group formative process." He suggests ten types of "central persons" or members who play key roles in the formation of a group. This is a typology of affective *roles*, more than one of which may be held by a group member, and is not merely a characterization of styles of "leadership." The typology is systematically derived from psychoanalytic conceptions of interpersonal relations. More by way of illustration than of explication, we may note that three of the role types (the patriarch, the Boy or Girl Scout troop leader type, and the tyrant —as Redl refers to them) derive from the central person's position "as an object of identification." This is in line with Freud's conception of group leadership. In two more role types the central person is an "object of drives," drives of love or aggression. A group united by a common love (for example, a fan club) would be an instance of the former; a group united by a common hatred (for example, an underground resistance movement), an instance of the latter. Finally, Redl describes five central person role types which serve as "ego supports" for members of the group. Actually, these may be said to be integrative (superego directed) or malintegrative (id directed) roles; they are subdivided on the basis of specific acts or general models. The roles Redl terms "The Bad Influence" and "The Good Example" represent these general models of id-oriented and superego-oriented behavior. Such central persons do not so much *do* something as they *stand for* something—in the one case, antisocial impulses, and in the other, moral impulses. In other words, such figures are symbolic and may play an important part in group life as living embodiments, as it were, of fundamental psychological tendencies or of basic moral values.

This brief sketch of two psychoanalytic contributions to our understanding of affective relationships in groups can scarcely qualify as an adequate treatment of the work of the two authors or of psychoanalytic thinking in general. The account is intended, rather, to suggest that the elucidation of internal networks of affective bonds need not be confined to the like/dislike dichotomies of sociometry. Empirically, the measurement of these more complex identifications faces very difficult obstacles, but at least in our theoretical formulations we ought to be prepared to think in more complex terms than sociometry permits.

Different as they are in their conception of the structure of feeling, or the network of affective relations, in a small group, both the sociometric and psychoanalytic approaches stress *expressive* rather than *instrumental* behavior and emphasize group structure rather than group process. That these emphases do not exhaust the possibilities of analyzing social structure is brought out by consideration of alternative methods of studying groups.

The Group as a Network of Communication

Some students of small groups have seen the crucial phenomenon of group life as consisting not of affect but of communication. Alex Bavelas, the most widely known representative of this approach, has posed the problem as follows:

> When the nature of a task is such that it must be performed by a group rather than by a single individual, the problem of working relationships arises. One of the more important of these relationships is that of communication. Quite aside from a consideration of the effects of communication on what is generally called "morale," it is easily demonstrated that for entire classes of tasks any hope of success depends upon an effective flow of information. But on what principles may a pattern of communication be determined which in fact will be a fit one for human effort? ... Do certain patterns have structural properties which may limit group performance? May it be that among several communication patterns—*all logically adequate for the successful completion of a specified task*—one will result in significantly better performance than another? What effects might pattern, as such, have upon the emergence of leadership, the development of organization, and the degree of resistance to group disruption?[8]

How can we go about finding answers to questions such as these? One way would be to observe a great many groups and to try to correlate degrees of efficiency with patterns of communication. Measuring efficiency should not prove too difficult, but how could we guarantee that the groups would develop *different* patterns of communication? One solution is to rely on chance to produce these variations over a series of group sessions.

A more direct approach involving experimental manipulation

of channels of communication has been followed by Bavelas and his coworkers. Deciding to focus on communication rather than on groups as such, Bavelas devised an experimental arrangement whereby subjects, separated by partitions, sent messages to one another by poking notes through slots or by pressing keys which caused lights to blink in neighboring booths. This procedure eliminated face-to-face spontaneity and volubility (and, no doubt, much "irrelevant" affectively toned interaction) but made it possible to arrange communication patterns experimentally. Moreover, it became possible to calculate exactly how many and what kind of messages were actually sent. These messages could then be correlated with such variables as problem difficulty, efficiency of solution, subject estimates of leadership, and job satisfaction.

The patterns of communication links which Bavelas and his colleagues chose for study in their five-man groups were fairly simple:

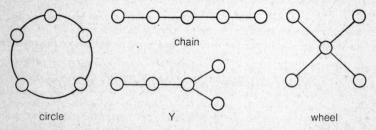

circle chain Y wheel

Differences were found among these patterns: ". . . the circle, one extreme, is active, leaderless, unorganized, erratic, and yet is enjoyed by its members. The wheel, at the other extreme, is less active, has a distinct leader, is well and stably organized, is less erratic, and yet is unsatisfying to most of its members."[9] Morale of members was largely a matter of centrality: those in the center of a communication network were more satisfied than those who were peripheral. In the circle, everyone is equally central (and equally likely to be rated "the leader" after the session), but in the wheel, one member is central and is always rated as leader. When the experimenter introduced a different group task requiring new procedures for its solution, the circle was able to adjust more quickly than was the highly organized wheel.

There are, obviously, other patterns of communication, other group sizes, other tasks, and additional variables—such as leadership style—which one might wish to investigate. Illustrative of some of these possibilities is the work of Marvin Shaw, who has studied various networks under authoritarian and democratic leadership. Using a somewhat more refined measure of centrality of position in the communication network (for which he used the term "independence"), he found close association with high morale and good performance. Too heavy a burden of communication imposed on a member (a condition he referred to as "saturation") was associated with low morale and poor performance. Thus, it seems, a member does best when he or she has freedom but, at the same time, not too crushing a task. In all networks studied, authoritarian leadership was resented and morale was low because the amount of "independence" was lower, but it produced better performance in problem-solving because, Shaw concludes, "saturation" is controlled by the authoritarian leader.[10] On the whole, these results support the conclusions reached by Lippitt and White in their study of group atmospheres.

Like this earlier study of group atmospheres, the studies of Bavelas and Shaw may claim to be dealing with analogies of social processes found in larger societies: there is an analogy between the circle and the "open" or democratic society on the one hand, and between the wheel and the "closed" or authoritarian society on the other. The value of these studies, therefore, lies not alone in their technical inventiveness but also in their ability to suggest how the study of the small group may help sharpen our perceptions and clarify hypotheses about types of societies. It is always an advantage in sociology to be made aware of underlying similarities in social forms and social processes as they occur in different contexts.

Some of these cultural differences in performance in communication networks are evident in a variation of the Leavitt experiment conducted by Hare in which Yoruba and Ibo students at the University of Ibadan in Nigeria were tested in four-man groups in two conditions: wheel network followed by circle network and circle network followed by wheel.[11] Their average number of messages sent, time, and satisfaction for each trial were compared with those of students who had participated in similar experiments at Haverford College in the United States, at the University of Cape Town in South Africa, and at three colleges in the Philippines.

The largest differences were between the U.S. groups and the Nigerian groups in the wheel and between the U.S. groups and the Philippine groups in the circle. The students in the U.S. groups sent fewer messages and took less time to solve the problems in both types of network and tended to give lower ratings on satisfaction when they were not in the center of the wheel. With the exception of the Yoruba in Nigeria, all groups sent fewer messages but took more time to solve the problems in the wheel than in the circle. In all nationality groups, the average member was more satisfied in the circle than in the noncentral positions in the wheel.

Nigerian groups apparently took longer to solve the problems, especially in the wheel, because they were more likely to interpret the task as one in which each individual should solve the problem alone rather than cooperate and accept the answer from another group member. Since this was not true at the University of Cape Town in South Africa, it was evident that the difference lay in a "non-European" approach to problem-solving, rather than in simply living on the continent of Africa.

In the Philippines, the greater number of messages in the circle and the higher level of satisfaction with the task both seemed to reflect a concern for "smooth interpersonal relations," which led group members to check continually the extent of their agreement and understanding and to inhibit the overt expression of negative comment.

Seating Position

For the communication-network experiments discussed up to this point, the communication net was *explicitly* imposed by the experimenter. But communication networks are also *implicit* in the seating arrangements in discussion groups and in other everyday settings, where they have similar effects on patterns of social interaction.[12] The overall seating arrangement that people choose is directly related to the task. If the task calls for face-to-face interaction in a group discussion, persons usually choose to sit relatively close together in a circle or in a semicircle facing the discussion leader. If only two people are involved, they sit opposite each other.

In a social session when there is no central task and conversations do not have to be heard by all, group members are more likely to turn to the person next to them for informal discussion. This is especially true if one member of the pair is a woman, and also in cafeterias or other informal settings, where members of a pair tend to choose seats at right angles at the corner of a table.

When privacy is desirable, as when one is studying in the library, eating alone in a restaurant, or using a public toilet, individuals have been observed choosing seats that provide for maximum privacy. If their personal space is invaded, they are likely to retreat. Individuals will also try to avoid invading another person's personal space even if the other person appears to be blocking their way.

It is customary for formal group leaders to occupy a position at the head of the conference table or some other clearly identified position. As a result, persons who wish to assume leadership in a group will tend to occupy the more central and visible positions, and those who occupy these positions, regardless of personal characteristics, will tend to become leaders.

The proximity of seating positions is clearly related to attraction. If individuals wish to come closer to each other emotionally, they tend to come closer physically, but not too close. If they wish to avoid someone, they leave an empty seat or select a seat that does not face another person.

The seat one chooses is only one indicator of the use of personal space. Whether one is seated, standing, or lying down, proximity and other aspects of body position provide nonverbal indicators of all dimensions of social interaction. In a typical experiment, the experimenter asks the subjects to come into an office for an interview and then notes how far away the subject stands or sits during the interview. In field observations, observers note how far apart people stand while waiting in queues, talking at parties, or lying on the beach. In general, individuals come closer if they have a positive relationship and keep their distance if they have a negative relationship or if there are marked status differences. Females are usually comfortable at closer distances than males, and ethnic groups differ in the distance for normal conversation.

In common with other animals, people become attached to a particular area and attempt to defend their territory from invaders. In children's groups, the defense may involve actual fighting, but adults may defend an area by using personal "markers." For example, a student in the library who wants to have a table alone may choose a central seat and then place books, sweaters, sandwiches, or other personal "markers" around the table to give the impression that the space is fully occupied.

GENERAL THEORIES

However crucial affectivity or communication may be in the life of groups and societies, they are still "special" in the sense that they deal with a particular facet of group relations. The more general theories claim to embrace all the features of group structure that are essential to a basic sociology of small groups. They do not thereby claim to have answered all the questions one might ask about small groups, but they do put forward frames of reference within which, they contend, the general sociology of groups may develop. The approaches to be discussed are those of George Homans, of the Group Dynamics school, and of Robert F. Bales.

Homans

In his book *The Human Group,*[13] Homans presents a framework simple in outline yet broad enough to encompass group life in slum gangs, factory teams, and South Sea Island families. The chief conceptual elements of this framework are *activity, sentiment, interaction,* and *norms;* they refer, respectively, to the operations people perform, the feelings they have, the communication they carry on, and the standards they uphold.* In addition, Homans, like many sociologists before him, distinguishes between the "external" and the "internal" system in groups:

> We may say that the *external system* is the state of these elements [activity, sentiment, and so forth] and of their interrelations, so far as it constitutes a solution—not necessarily the only possible solution—of the problem: How shall the group survive in its environment? We call it external because it is conditioned by the environment; we call it a system because in it the elements of behavior are mutually dependent. The external system, plus another set of relations which we shall call the *internal system,* make up the total social system.[14]

This internal system is

> not directly conditioned by the environment, ... we speak of it as an "elaboration" because it includes forms of behavior not included under the heading of the external system. We shall not go far wrong if ... we ... think of the internal system as group behavior that is an expression of the sentiments towards one another developed by the members of the group in the course of their life together.[15]

These, then, are the analytical elements of Homans' system. Essentially, he is concerned to show that they are mutually influential variables. He adduces evidence from a series of natural (and in a later study[16] experimental) groups to support such hypotheses as the following:

> The more frequently persons interact with one another, the stronger their sentiments of friendship for one another are apt to be.[17]

*When referring to norms of a more far-reaching, ideal, and deep-seated variety (such as "democracy"), Homans uses the term *values.*

> Persons who interact with one another frequently are more like one another in their activities than they are like other persons with whom they interact less frequently.[18]

> To the degree that the activities of the other individual in a reciprocal role relationship conform to the norms of one's own group, one will like him.[19]

Focusing more closely on group process, Homans suggests generalizations about two important phenomena found in groups, rank differentiation and leadership:

> The higher a member's rank, the more often he originates interaction as well as the more often he receives it.[20]

> The more nearly equal in social rank a number of men are, the more frequently they will interact with one another.[21]

> The closer a member comes to realizing the norms of the group, the more interactions he will receive from and give to other members of the group.... One can call the member who comes *closest* and interacts *most* the leader....[22]

Such hypotheses do not by any means exhaust Homans' formulations, but will serve as examples of the type of generalization possible within his frame of analysis.

As Homans himself repeatedly asserts, all this represents only a first step: he has affirmed that major parts of group life are interrelated, but the generalizations are still too sweeping to be entirely satisfactory. Their inadequacy may be said to stem from two sources: the absence of precise measurement of the variables and the failure to distinguish subelements or components within the broad variables of activity, interaction, and so forth.

On the first of these difficulties, Homans himself has written:

> If a system of hypotheses is to account for, and ultimately to predict, the actual behavior of a group, the hypotheses themselves are not enough. We must also be able to assign values to the elements entering the hypotheses.... We have not been able to assign values to the elements.... We have solved the problem only comparatively, in terms of less or more, not how much less

or more. Progress in this direction will have to wait for the development of measurements through which we will be able to assign values to the elements of behavior and get comparable results from group to group.[23]

The assertion that Homans' system does not distinguish the "subelements" within the "variables" means that *sentiment*, for instance, is too gross a category to be very helpful, and that rather than worry about more accurate sociometric measurement of likes and dislikes, we ought to be worrying about whether likes and dislikes constitute the only thing we mean (or *ought* to mean) by "sentiment." It might be argued that this is a problem of measurement, but that would be to use "measurement" as synonymous with clarification and the process of abstracting out crucial features of the total situation. Again, perhaps the most important question is not whether interaction varies with, say, activity, but rather what forms of interaction humans employ and how these forms can be adequately categorized so as to be subject to their interrelationships to experimental verification. Or again—and this point has been raised before —we are less interested in hearing that norms influence behavior than in learning about the content of the norms that typically operate in group life and about the conditions under which they do so in one way rather than in another.

In short, the criticism that can be made of Homans' approach is not that it is untrue or even that it is limited in its applicability, but that it does not take us very far. It does not carry us much beyond the notion that human behavior (in its broadest sense) somehow hangs together, that its parts do relate one to another, that what people do affects who they know and how they feel (though no priority attaches to the doing or the feeling or to any of the other major components). If we are unfamiliar with this conception of interdependence, Homans' treatment is as clear and logical as any that has been written and thus serves an admirable purpose. But it is by no means to be assumed that the best road to reality, as we apprehend it intuitively from our experience, is necessarily the most direct one—that is to say, that those aspects which present themselves most readily to the naked eye will necessarily turn out to be most useful in disclosing the basic nature of things. One of the more mischievous temptations in the path of wisdom is the assumption that the appropriate categories are given—lying right there on the surface—and are amenable to investigation by anyone who has the interest and the energy— that the materials with which we work are provided by the management, so to speak, and our job is simply to arrange them.

This criticism of Homans, to be sure, takes a pretty high line and ignores the fact that there are legitimate alternatives in social science. Nevertheless, it is a criticism that ought to be raised with reference to any approach to the study of social behavior.

Group Dynamics

Group Dynamics is the most widespread and influential current approach to the study of group behavior.* Its founder and guid- ing spirit was the social psychologist Kurt Lewin. Emigrating from Nazi Germany, Lewin established centers for psychologi- cal research at the University of Iowa and at Massachusetts Institute of Technology. His colleagues, former students, and followers are now to be found in almost all the major centers of small-group research in this country, most notably perhaps at the Research Center for Group Dynamics at the University of Mich- igan.[25]

The Perspective. The perspective of Group Dynamics, generally speaking, is that of Gestalt psychology, the emphasis being on wholes or totalities as distinguished from particular stimuli and particular responses. It involves a conception of a *field* of forces (indeed, the Lewinian–Group Dynamics approach is sometimes referred to as "Field Theory") that play upon and influence the

*The term "group dynamics" is often used as roughly synonymous with "the study of small groups"; in this study, the capitalized term refers to a particular conception of group analysis and not to the field as a whole.

The problem of doing justice to the wealth of empirical investigations carried on under the banner of Group Dynamics is particularly acute. The aim here is not to summarize findings but to elucidate theoretical substructure. Reprintings and summaries of much of the original research are readily available.[24]

various subparts or elements within the field. As a prominent exponent of Group Dynamics has written:

> This method, in a manner analogous to that of field theory in physics, assumes that the properties of any event are determined by its relations to the system of events of which it is a component. . . .
>
> All psychological events (thinking, acting, dreaming, hoping, etc.) are conceived to be a function of the life space which consists of the person and the environment viewed as *one* constellation of interdependent factors. That is, all psychological events are conceived to be determined, not by isolated properties of the person or his environment, but by the mutual relations among the totality of coexisting facts which comprise the life space. . . .[26]

This way of looking at things is now pretty much a part of what we might call the social science frame of reference, owing in no small part to Lewin (and also, among other influences, to functionalism in sociology and social anthropology). As an ideal it is unassailable: we should be cognizant of *all* the factors. In practice, however, it leaves unanswered the question of *how* we are to take all the factors into account, or short of this, *which* factors seem to be especially worth investigating. The various fields of social science have again and again foundered on this practical question—and Group Dynamics is a case in point.

The Symbolic System. A perspective or point of view requires a detailed set of symbols for defining and structuring the total field it seeks to encompass. The symbolic or notational system developed by Lewin for social psychological research is drawn from physics to some extent but more notably from non-Euclidean geometry. Lewin's earlier researches were called "Studies in Topological and Vector Psychology," reflecting his interest in the branch of modern mathematics known as topology (which deals with such relations of bodies as inclusion and exclusion, adjacency and nonadjacency, rather than with the points, lines, and planes of Euclidean geometry). Lewin found this a useful way of conceptualizing the relations of a part to a whole or the movement of an individual through his or her life space. This topological mode of conceptualization gave rise to a frequent use of maplike diagrams in which subsections of the life space are signified by lines of various thickness and permeability. A profusion of algebraic-like letters and subscripts adds to the complexity and scientific appearance of the diagrams. In sum, the thought model or image is spatial rather than, say, organic or mechanical.

Such topological or diagrammatic representations are coming to be recognized as metaphors, helpful to people who are helped by this sort of metaphor. But they do not really enable us to state motivational change "in a geometrically precise manner," as Lewin claimed,[27] any more than a photograph of group activity shows motivation in a chemically precise manner. They are, in one psychologist's words, "not much more than diagrammatic representations of his brilliant theoretical and experimental insights."[28] Diagrams of Lewinian proportions are largely absent from recent work in Group Dynamics, but Lewin's concern for precise ways of formulating relationships and hypotheses has had a continuing and beneficial effect on his followers. It is one of the identifying characteristics of the Group Dynamics approach that it is at special pains to be as logical and exact as possible in specifying the connections between propositions.

The Key Research Concepts.   In descriptions of research in Group Dynamics, one finds such terms as *locomotion, valence, vector, cohesiveness, powerfield,* and *group forces.* The picture of group life is one in which a member or a group locomotes ("any change of position of any region within the life space is conceived to be a locomotion")[29] toward regions having positive valences (attraction) and away from those having negative valences (repulsion). In other words, goal-seeking behavior is postulated. The direction of this behavior (its vector) reflects the contending powerfields and group forces which induce changes in behavior.

All this is conceptual rather than substantive; it represents the rudiments of a language for use in investigation rather than the findings of empirical study. This does not make such concepts any less significant, for any set of concepts, be it that of Group Dynamics or psychoanalysis or Marxism, predisposes its user to see some aspects of "reality" and to be blinded to other aspects: such is the nemesis of all our attempts at objectivity.

A good part of the research in Group Dynamics has centered around the two problems of *cohesiveness* and *locomotion*.

One widely quoted definition of *cohesiveness* is "the total field of forces which act on members to remain in the group."[30] This definition is in keeping with the broad "field" perspective described above. In practice, as distinguished from theory, cohesiveness is customarily defined in terms of sociometric friendship choices (for instance, in the study from which the above definition comes, cohesiveness is measured by responses to the question "What three people do you see most of socially?"). Other characteristics of groups may also be interpreted as measures of cohesiveness: the frequency with which members say "we" as compared to "I," the extent to which they share norms, or the rate of absenteeism.

Treating cohesiveness as a dependent variable, we may note briefly some of the conditions (independent variables) which have been shown to affect it. Making for a greater degree of cohesiveness are: an emphasis on cooperation rather than competition, a democratic as distinguished from an authoritarian or laissez-faire group atmosphere; the existence of previous organization in the group; and membership in a persistently high status group (that is, one more rewarded by the experimenter) or even "central" membership in a persistently low status group (one insulted and rejected by the experimenter). If the status of the group changes for worse or for better, cohesiveness is lessened.[31] Cohesiveness has been shown to be a product of liking another member (this would appear to be largely tautological), of group prestige, and of task interest.[32] Such other variables as the similarities among members, structural properties, and group size also have an effect.[33]

Considering cohesiveness in this manner—that is, as an independent variable—we may note some of its consequences. Members of cohesive groups tend to be more attentive to one another, more open to change and to influence, and more likely to internalize the group's norms (though one study found that cohesiveness was influential only in *reducing* a group's productivity and not in increasing it).[34] Cohesive groups are more friendly and tend to stand up better under frustration.[35] Cohesiveness is one of the factors making for uniformity in the attitudes and behavior of group members.[36]

The concept of *locomotion* applies to the group as a whole as well as to its individual members. To proceed to a common goal, a group must communicate and must have some degree of cohesiveness. That is, a group which has to overcome obstacles to its task solution must have some mutually binding element (though it should not be assumed that group productivity will necessarily correlate with degree of friendliness among members). One such obstacle to group locomotion is the presence of members who do not go along with the majority view and who thus prevent the necessary unanimity. Experimental studies, using stooges who purposely put themselves in this "deviate" role, show that communication tends to be directed toward the deviate in an effort to get him to change.[37] Where unanimity is not required, rejection of the deviate becomes a likely pattern.[38]

In one experiment, "status" differences were established by pairing a series of groups: one group in each pair was told it had the better and more important job in the joint solution of a problem with the other group; the latter was told it had the more menial and routine role. Actually, the two jobs were the same. The induced status differences were found to reduce the amount of communication between the two status groups as they locomoted to their problem solution. The pattern of specifically *critical* communication was also affected by these status differences. "The existence of hierarchy [status] produces restraining forces against communicating criticisms of persons at the other level. High status seems to give persons greater freedom to express whatever criticism they have of the other level directly to the criticized person rather than to one's own level."[39] If the low-status group is promoted to high status, "these groups show what appears to be a cathartic discharge of aggressive communication against the opposing groups.... However, if instead of successful upward mobility, the group action is repulsed by the experimenter, then the discharge of aggressive communication tends to decrease from an already moderate rate. . . ."[40]

When locomotion is conceived of as applying to the individual member within the group (rather than to the group as a whole), the complexity of the problem increases and the number of research findings decreases. This is because we are now dealing with a differentiated entity, with the different positions or functions which group members fill—in other words, with social structure. In its treatment of social structure, Group Dynamics can point to auspicious beginnings in the Lippitt and White investigations of styles of group leadership. Curiously enough, these have not developed into a concerted series of studies on the sources and functions of various types of leadership. Rather, research interest has tended to diffuse into the pursuit of a wide variety of member roles, roles which happen to be of interest to this or that investigator but whose *general* significance for group life is often not clear. "Resource persons," "recognition seekers," "procedural technicians," "gate-keepers," and so forth are recognizable role types, but they do not derive from an explicit conception of the positions or dimensions of differentiation to be found in groups. The dimensions tend to be ad hoc, worked out in connection with a particular project but not built into Field Theory or into long-range research programs. Citing some of the studies mentioned above, one student of Group Dynamics concludes that

> the concepts of *group structure* and of *position within the group* have not been well defined in the writings of group dynamicists. . . . The very diversity of these studies indicates some of the varied meanings that the term "position" may have. "Position" has been employed to refer to the functions a member performs in a group, to an individual's locus in a communication network, to a person's ability to induce forces, to a person's prestige in the group, etc. . . . to characterize adequately any group member's relations to others in the group over a period of time and in different social settings one will have to locate him along a number of dimensions, i.e. in a number of different positions.[41]

This criticism suggests that Group Dynamics could profit from more systematic, and deductive, thinking about the essential roles to be found in all groups. The original work in democratic, laissez-faire, and authoritarian styles of leadership represents a step in this direction, but despite its ready acceptance by Field Theorists and others interested in better human relations, it has not been followed by work of equal caliber or significance.[42]

Let us return once more to the two major concepts with which students of Group Dynamics have chosen to work. The concept of locomotion may be interpreted as Group Dynamics' chief intellectual device for dealing with task- or problem-oriented activity in the group. It is generally treated as a characteristic of groups rather than of individuals; group process is thus represented as a movement toward or away from the successful achievement of the group's agenda. Since there is little theory to indicate what is relevant to successful task accomplishment and what is not, the common-sense judgments by group members and by observers as to what constitutes locomotion must be viewed with some caution. Those aspects of group process that do not *appear* to be relevant are either neglected as outside the purview of the science of groups or associated with the concept of cohesiveness.

Cohesiveness, then, may be interpreted as one way of conceptualizing affective, noninstrumental behavior. It is usually pictured as a "force" operating in a group to make it solidary; sometimes it is conceived as a result of a "total field of forces" —that is, as the condition of being solidary. In practice, it is usually measured by sociometric friendship choices. Furthermore, cohesiveness is customarily treated as a group characteristic and is measured by averaging the friendship ratings of the group's members. If, however, we recognize that there are differences among members with respect to functions, positions, or roles, the possibility arises that some people's choosings may be more important than others. In this connection, Cartwright and Zander write:

> The simplest formulation of group cohesiveness would be that it equals the sum of the resultant forces on members to remain

in the group. Each member would be given equal weight. A formulation essentially of this type has been used in most of the research conducted up to the present, and on the whole it has proved satisfactory. There can hardly be any doubt, however, that the degree to which certain members are attracted to the group makes a critical difference, while the degree of attraction of other members is relatively inconsequential to the group.[43]

Several further questions arise in connection with the concept of cohesiveness. Are there not, possibly, varieties of cohesiveness? Might these not come from different sources and have different consequences? Moreover, in what manner has Group Dynamics taken into account the familiar sociological distinction between primary and secondary forms of group solidarity? Occasionally these problems are touched upon by students of Group Dynamics, but they have not received the explicit treatment they would appear to demand.[44]

To reiterate a point made earlier: the fact that it is possible to see behavior in terms of certain categories does not insure that these categories will be the most fruitful ones to employ. The history of scientific inquiry is strewn with the wreckage of once-fashionable but ultimately inadequate categories and conceptual models—from the four elements of fire, air, earth, and water to the concepts of force and of immutable natural law. Enthusiasm, seriousness, and a fondness for mathematics do not a science make. What is required, of course, is a knowledge of what to look for and an understanding of how the variables selected for observation constitute the framework of a functioning whole. This is a big order, and one which none of us is prepared to fill. Grim pursuit of a few handy variables on the one hand, or essentially wistful talk about "total fields" on the other, do not quite measure up to this implacable demand.

In sum, the achievements of Group Dynamics include its concern for carefully formulated hypotheses, the large amount of interest it has aroused in group behavior, and its findings, which spell out in detail some relationships which we might otherwise have only suspected. Its limitations lie in the inadequacy and probable inappropriateness of its working-level concepts and in its failure to pay attention to what non-Lewinian thinking might have to suggest as to major problems or variables in group life —especially with reference to the dimensions of role differentiation.

Interaction Process Analysis

Interaction Process Analysis is the theory and method of small-group research developed by Robert F. Bales of the Harvard Laboratory of Social Relations.

The Perspective.   The starting point, as well as the goal, of Interaction Process Analysis is the process of problem-solving. Inspired in part by the pragmatism of John Dewey, Bales conceives of all group activity as being problem-solving activity. This conception applies equally to affective or expressive behavior and to more overtly goal-directed or task-oriented behavior. Thus, in theory, every item of behavior should be fitted into some structural category, and none of it should be treated residually. It is evident that Interaction Process Analysis shares a basic tenet of Field Theory: the intention of treating total situations and not merely a selection of particular stimuli and particular responses.

In place of the explicit spatial metaphor of Group Dynamics, an implicit image of the *flow* of process is more characteristic of Bales' thinking. Bales suggests that the process of interaction be conceived of as a continual stream of acts, words, symbols, reactions, gestures, and so forth. This stream may flow quickly and smoothly, or it may flow slowly; it may break off altogether or become so fragmented that a "mending" process must take place if communication is to continue at all. This stream flows from member to member and back again, sometimes including all and sometimes only part of the group, with the result that the various channels of communication may be very unevenly employed. Interaction, then, is thought of as being distributed over time and among persons. It is also conceived of as varying in type—questions, statements of fact, emotional outbursts, and so on.

To complement the activist-pragmatist image of a natural tendency to problem-solving, there is another element in Bales' thinking, one which might be referred to as the "uncertainty principle." This principle in effect states that any change means the disturbance of a status quo, the upsetting of an equilibrium —an uncertainty to which the members of the group must adjust. Thus in addition to being viewed as a collection of eager doers, the group is seen as a collection of suspicious resisters, to whom any act is a potential threat. This may help to explain the amount of attention Bales has given to the internal problems of rivalry and tension in groups.

> Even in cases of successful solution of the sub-problems [Bales writes] we assume that there is a "wear and tear" involved ... which demands periodic activity oriented more or less directly to the problem of distributing the rewards accruing from productive activity back to individual members of the system and re-establishing their feeling of solidarity or integration with it. In particular we believe that the necessities of control or modification of activity in order to control the outer situation productively is likely to *put the existing integration of the system under strain, no matter how successful* the attack on the situational problem may eventually be.[45]

This brings us to a fundamental feature of Interaction Process Analysis, its treatment of social structure. The patterning of social relationships is not merely an empirical fact of group life; as the direct outgrowth of the situation just described, it is related theoretically to the fundamental tendencies of human behavior. Bales describes this connection as follows:

> The actions of other individuals ... are always relevant to the problems of tension reduction of any given individual. ... It is to the advantage of every individual in a group to stabilize the potential activity of others toward him favorably if possible, but in any case in such a way that he can predict it. ... All of them, even those who may wish to exploit the others, have some interest in bringing about stability. A basic assumption here is that what we call the "social structure" of groups can be understood primarily as a system of solutions to the functional problems of interaction which become institutionalized in order to reduce the

tensions growing out of uncertainty and unpredictability in the actions of others.[46]

To meet this presumably basic human need for predictability, a structure of roles develops. This occurs even in laboratory groups.

How are we to characterize this phenomenon of social structure other than to say it answers fundamental needs? In seeking "the most general or universal kinds of differentiations which exist or develop between persons . . . in small groups," Bales discerns four dimensions or axes of role differentiation which, taken together, are said to constitute the group's social structure. These dimensions are the differential degree of (1) access to resources, (2) control over persons, (3) status in a stratified scale of importance or prestige, and (4) solidarity or identification with the group as a whole.[47]

1. Access to resources. This dimension represents an attempt to account for the fact that individuals vary with respect to their possession of things (resources) that the group considers important or valuable. Writes Bales:

> Freedom from control, the possession of time, physical objects, and specific services are all either resources to further goals or goals in themselves which are possessed in varying degrees by members of the group and which can be given or withheld. . . . Any resource which is not unlimited, or which may be divided among persons, or which in its nature is such that as one person has more another automatically has less, may require stabilization of activity related to its distribution in order to prevent insecurity or deprivation on the part of the disadvantaged members.[48]

One variety of member role, then, is definable in terms of an individual's access to resources. The result is a structure that, in larger social systems, is referred to as the structure of property relations.

2. Control over persons. This is the dimension of authority in small groups.

> Both from the fact that persons *can* control each other by force or coercion and from the fact that they *need* to control each other because of complicated divisions of labor addressed to problem solution arise pressures for some kind of regularization or institutionalization of the control relations between persons. In every group the observer expects to find at least *pressures* toward a stabilization of control of persons over others.[49]

The threat of a disruptive struggle for power and the need for integration in the pursuit of common ends, therefore, provide the *raison d'être* for a system of authority.

3. Status. The structure of status relationships is said to be relative to the individual's contribution to the group goal.

> Every individual ... who is concerned with the reaching of goals will be impelled to evaluate other persons in terms of how they relate to the achievement of these goals and in terms of whether their activity tends to maintain or destroy the norms upon which emotional safety depends. . . . If and when a basic consensus as to the proper status order of persons is established in the group, the group may be said to be stratified.[50]

4. Solidarity. This aspect of social structure is defined in terms of the individual's place in a network of mutual loyalties and affection.

> The heart of solidarity in the institutionalized sense is the stabilized mutual responsibility of each toward the other to regard himself as part of the other, as the sharer of a common fate, and as a person who is under obligation to cooperate with the other in the satisfaction of the other's individual needs as if they were one's own. Solidarity in certain of its aspects is a quality of social relationships which tends to arise spontaneously. It does not necessarily arise *because* it has an instrumental value in the problem-solving process for each—it is in part an unpremeditated result of the expression of affect toward others and inclusion in an in-group—but the fact that it exists has an instrumental value for each, and the preserving and maintaining of it has an instrumental as well as an expressive value.[51]

These, then, are the dimensions that define social structure. They are not empirical findings but rather theoretical derivatives that arise from what Bales calls "the most generalized features of the process of action." They form part of a theoretical model of group behavior and represent analogies to kinds of role differentiation found in large-scale societies.

The Method. Interaction Process Analysis shares many of the research techniques employed by other approaches: the isolation of the observer behind a one-way mirror; the use of tape recorders, sociometric questionnaires, statistical treatment of data; and so forth. Its distinguishing feature is a set of categories in terms of which the observer records group process. These categories represent an extension and systematization of observational techniques employed by earlier investigators—for instance, Lippitt and White, who noted the I/we ratio, the frequency of hostile remarks, and so forth. In Bales' method the observer records (on a moving tape) who says what to whom in terms of one of twelve types of interaction. The observer does not write down a summary of conversation; rather, the observer indicates into which category a remark falls—for example, whether it is a request for information, a suggestion for procedure, a disagreement, or whatever. The twelve categories in Bales' system were not built up inductively as the occasion seemed to demand, but were deduced from what were conceived to be the essential properties of the interactive problem-solving system as represented by the small group. Originally, Bales drew up a list of some eighty-seven types of acts involved in the problem-solving process. In the desire to create a list that would have some usefulness in empirical research, these eighty-seven were subsequently reduced to thirty-two categories, then to fourteen, and finally to twelve.

Figure 3 presents the set of twelve categories in standard abbreviated form. It will be noted, first of all, that the set embodies the instrumental versus affective (or task orientation versus group orientation) distinction: areas B and C are referred to as "task areas," while A and D are referred to as "social-emotional areas." Within the task area is included not only the "asks for" and "gives" distinction but also the ancient tripartite distinction

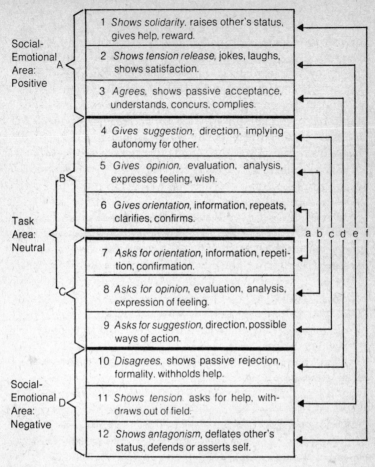

KEY

a   Problems of Communication   d   Problems of Decision
b   Problems of Evaluation   e   Problems of Tension Reduction
c   Problems of Control   f   Problems of Reintegration

A   Positive Reactions   C   Questions
B   Attempted Answers   D   Negative Reactions

FIGURE 3. Bales' System of Observational Categories

Source: Robert F. Bales, *Interaction Process Analysis* (Chicago: University of Chicago Press, 1950), p. 9. © 1950 by The University of Chicago. A revised version of these categories is given in Bales, *Personality and Interpersonal Behavior* (New York: Holt, Rinehart and Winston, 1970).

between thinking, feeling, and willing—categories 6 and 7, 5 and 8, and 4 and 9 respectively. Within the social-emotional areas the breakdown of categories is roughly in terms of degree of emotionality: mild agreement or disagreement in categories 3 and 10, overt praise or insults in categories 1 and 12. Areas A and D deal most directly (though not exclusively) with acts relevant to the "internal" situation, the power struggle and the currents of friendship and hostility; areas B and C deal most directly (though again not exclusively) with acts relevant to the "external" situation—that is, the group's task insofar as it involves the manipulation of symbols in conversation.

In any such observational system, there are problems of validity and reliability: does it encompass meaningful aspects of group process, and does it do so in the same fashion for all observers? The former question can be answered only by reviewing research that employs this method. First, however, we may note two interrelated assumptions of Bales' method. One assumption is that the set of categories is exhaustive at its chosen level of abstraction. The procedure deliberately neglects much of what we know is important—the content of what is said or the quality of suggestions made—while nevertheless claiming that every act has a place within the scheme, a place defined by the functions of the act in the problem-solving process. Second, the practice of scoring each act in terms of a single category runs counter to what experience tells us: that a remark may serve several purposes or functions—that it may, for example, supply information and at the same time refute an opponent. The recording procedure of Interaction Process Analysis rests on the assumptions that the observer can judge the dominant function or meaning of an act, and that in the long run the true tendencies of individual and group behavior will be portrayed with acceptable accuracy even though in any given instance the subsidiary function of the act will be lost. If this assumption is rejected, the observational method loses much of its significance.

The question of reliability is a technical one beyond the scope of this study, but it may be pointed out that Bales and his associates argue that the agreement between different observers using the twelve-category method is adequate for most purposes.[52] As long as one does not try to rest too weighty a conclusion on too unreliable a type of data (the estimate of remarks received, for instance, is notably unreliable) the observational technique is the most refined and the most exhaustive that has been so far developed for the analysis of small groups. It should not, of course, be assumed that by virtue of its detail this technique necessarily gets at basic, as distinguished from superficial, aspects of group activity.

In sum, we have a systematically conceived set of observational categories useful in the analysis of any sort of discussion group. It has been used extensively by Bales and his associates and has provided much data upon which to base generalizations about many problems of group behavior.

Some Problems Which Have Been Investigated

Profiles. The simplest way of presenting data obtained from the twelve-category recording system is in individual and group profiles. A profile is a straightforward summary of how much an individual—or all individuals—in a group gives and receives in the various categories; it can be portrayed numerically or graphically. Inspection of group profiles can show differences between types of groups—children's groups, adult groups, therapy groups,[53] "satisfied" and "unsatisfied" groups,[54] and so forth. Inspection of individual profiles can show that those who talk most in a group tend to have a different pattern of communicative behavior from those who talk least. Just what these differences are is not so easily ascertained. It would obviously be misleading to make very much of the fact that "high output" members laugh more than do "low output" members; by definition, the former indulge in all types of activity more than do the latter. Students of the subject are still in some disagreement as to how group members who differ in total quantity of output differ in the type and pattern of their responses.[55]

Channels of Communication. Data on quantity of output and intake provide information on problems similar to those investigated by Bavelas and his coworkers. When all the potential channels of communication are left open—as they are in a face-to-face discussion group—the amount of give-and-take is never equal for all members. Not only is output unequal, but a rank ordering of output and intake emerges, in which a member tends to give activity to other members in proportion to the output rank of the receivers and to receive activity from others in proportion to the output rank of the initiators.[56] Even without any artificial barriers to communication imposed by the experimenter, a tendency to centralization of communication is discernible.

> As groups increase in size, a larger and larger relative proportion of the activity tends to be addressed to the top man, and a smaller and smaller relative proportion to other members. In turn, as size increases, the top man tends to address more and more of his remarks to the group as a whole, and to exceed by larger amounts his proportions to share. The communication pattern tends to "centralize," in other words, around a leader through whom most of the communication flows.[57]

Phase Movement. By arranging data by temporal period or phase of the group session, it is possible to compare the kinds of activity which take place during, say, the first, second, and last thirds of a group meeting. Research employing these procedures shows that, under specified conditions,

> groups tend to move in their interaction from a relative emphasis upon problems of *orientation* [categories 6 and 7 in Figure 1], to problems of *evaluation* [categories 5 and 8], and subsequently to problems of *control* [categories 4 and 9], and that concurrent with these transitions, the relative frequencies of both *negative reactions* [categories 10 and 11 and 12] and *positive reactions* [categories 1 and 2 and 3] tend to increase.[58]

Role Relationships. The delineation of the major group roles and the investigation of their interrelationships constitute perhaps the most important line of inquiry that can be undertaken within any research tradition. It is one upon which Bales and his coworkers have focused almost exclusively in recent years.

In his earlier theoretical writings, Bales hypothesized that, in all social systems, roles relative to property ("access to resources"), authority, status, and solidarity are in a state of uneasy equilibrium, so that changes along one dimension tend to produce changes along the other dimensions. Thus, for instance, Bales suggested that

> as the felt advantage of a particular person in the distribution of access to resources increases, strains are created toward an increase in his generalized social status. . . . as status differences between persons increase, strains are created toward a less solid (more neutral, indifferent, or antagonistic) relation between them. . . .[59]

And again:

> As solidarity between persons performing specific, differentiated and formal roles increases, strains are created toward a more diffuse, less differentiated, and less formalized performance of functional social roles, which in turn may be accompanied by a loss of efficiency and responsibility, a loss of the inducement of increased status, a perversion of function from group ends to the individual ends of the persons immediately involved, and so may threaten the adaptation and integration of the group as a whole. (Nepotism, favoritism, particularism, etc.)[60]

In general, Bales concludes:

> The social system in its organization, we postulate, tends to swing or falter indeterminately back and forth between these two theoretical poles: optimum adaptation to the outer situation at the cost of internal malintegration, or optimum internal integration at the cost of maladaptation to the outer situation.[61]

Thus, according to this view, group life is characterized by an external or task aspect on the one hand and by an internal or social aspect on the other. Moreover, these aspects are inseparably united and are not merely disparate phenomena that happen to be present in group life. Furthermore, their interrelationship is, at bottom, one of rivalry and antagonism. In metaphysical terms, they constitute a Yin and Yang in eternal interdependent opposition.

How has later empirical investigation borne out these theoretical formulations? Though the general point of view has received some support, the more specific hypotheses have not been confirmed in any very precise way. The reason for this appears to be the difficulty of defining operationally the dimensions—access to resources, authority, status, and solidarity.

Figure 4 outlines alternative definitions of major types of roles. In the left-hand column is the tripartite distinction of Max Weber which is familiar to students of social stratification. The center column shows the theoretical bases of role differentiation that have previously been described—so far, a plausible correspondence. The right-hand column shows the *empirically* based types of roles which Bales and his associates are currently using. "Talking" is a label for amount of participation regardless of category. Considerable evidence and no little logic suggest that the ability to "hold the floor" in a discussion is a measure of one's access to those scarce resources, time and the attention of others. Sheer volume of communication has been found by many investigators to correlate well with the attribution of "leadership." For such reasons, the member with the highest participation or output is said to hold the "Talking" role. The "Ideas," "Guidance," and "Liking" roles are defined sociometrically—that is, by group members in response to such questions as "Who do you think had the best ideas?" "Who do you think did most to guide the group's discussion?" and "Whom did you like best?"

Two comments are in order concerning these latter three roles. First, they do not exhaust or even correspond very precisely to the theoretical distinctions. Though Bales has not explicitly made the associations, it seems fair to say that the "Ideas" role (that of the member acknowledged by other members to have contributed the best ideas) represents a disproportionate degree of access to a resource (good ideas) valuable to the group. The "Guidance" role may be said to represent both Authority and Prestige, depending on whether the evaluator interprets the question as asking for "the person who ran things" or "the person

Weber: bases of stratification.	IPA: theoretical bases of role differentiation.	IPA: empirical bases of role differentiation.
Class	Access to resources (Property)	Talking Ideas
Power	Control over persons (Authority)	Guidance
Status	Status (Prestige)	Guidance
——	Solidarity	Liking

FIGURE 4.   Alternative Definitions of Major Role Types

who promoted group goals." The "liking" role of the sociometrically most popular person is closer to Solidarity than to any of the other dimensions, though it can scarcely be said to constitute a very satisfactory operational definition of that phenomenon.

Second, the Ideas, Guidance, and Liking roles (and even the Talking role in part) are defined without reference to the elaborate observational system embodied in the twelve categories. Is it not curious that such an elegant method of recording behavior should be neglected or downgraded in favor of simple sociometric procedures? There appears to be a shift from what a theory suggests is important to what is experimentally convenient.

The shift took place for the same reason that most people compromise with reality: they cannot get where they want by sticking to the old rules. Originally, Bales had hoped that by devising indices from various combinations and ratios of categories he could obtain operational definitions of the major role types as these were suggested by his theory. This proved to be tedious and unpromising, but the evaluations or ratings made by group members turned out to be relatively quick and illuminating.

In Group Dynamics, we saw an instance of a premature closure of a theoretical system involving a few variables too common-sensical and yet too murky to permit a very sensitive penetration of the complexities of group life. In Interaction Process Analysis, we have, perhaps, an instance of the premature closure of a research technique involving a set of categories too elaborate and too unreliable for validating the conception of role structure with which it is associated. In this case, the desire to push deeper into the fundamentals of group behavior took precedence over the arranging and rearranging of the vast quantities of data and has led to placing the technique—at least temporarily and in part—in cold storage.

This shift of attention from technique to role structure has, on the whole, confirmed rather than vitiated the general point of view embodied in Interaction Process Analysis. It has been shown that the task roles of Ideas and Guidance are not usually held by the same group member who holds the social role of Liking. The separation or differentiation of these two types of roles (task and social) generally proceeds as the group process continues and the group, as we say, "develops." Talking, or output, is associated with Ideas and Guidance but not with Liking, which leads Bales to conclude that "there must be something about high participation and specialization in the technical [Idea] and executive [Guidance] directions which tends to provoke hostility."[62] This opposition between popularity and authority conforms to Bales' earlier line of thinking as well as to evidence from other sorts of social systems. It is at loggerheads with the notion mentioned earlier, in the discussion of sociometry, that popularity is tantamount to leadership. "Leadership"—as that quality is attributed by group members—is found by Bales to be associated less with sociometric liking than with any other of the roles he distinguishes: the "leader" role coincides with the Talking role in 50 percent of the cases studied, with Ideas in 59 percent of the cases, with Guidance in 79 percent of the cases, and with Liking in only 14 percent of the cases.[63]

In Bales' view, leadership is best conceived of not as a single role but as applying to several roles: Ideas, Guidance, and oddly enough, Liking. To put it somewhat differently, a well-organized group in which leadership functions are being satisfactorily performed involves an alliance between the "task specialist" and the "social-emotional specialist."

> In the small task-oriented group [Bales writes], positive affect is a scarce resource, and the practical problem, usually, is to find enough of it, and keep enough of it centered on the task specialist, either directly, or indirectly through the social leader, so that he does not lose power. . . . Centering their positive affect on another person, who in turn supports the task specialist, is a possible adjustment, and, we think, a rather common one. The social-emotional specialist, if this is a part of his role, is thus a kind of symbolic transmuter of negative affect into positive affect. His support of the task leader becomes a critical condition of the stability of the group.[64]

These generalizations, as Bales suggests, not only describe a basic feature of experimental group process, but also characterize the nuclear family in our society, wherein the father represents the "task specialist" and the mother the "social-emotional specialist." The applicability of small-group analysis to the study of the family (conceived of as one type of small group) and vice versa has become one of the major interests of Bales and his colleagues.

Bales' Three Dimensions of Social Evaluation

Although Bales' original category system is still the most widely used method for the analysis of interaction in small groups, Bales himself has gone on to summarize his theoretical perspective in terms of three dimensions of social evaluation.[65] Bales has now come out from behind the one-way mirror in the sociology laboratory and has given up the observer's role. He now takes his place inside the classroom as a trainer in a self-analytic group. His primary concern is no longer to provide a set of categories for professional social scientists to use in their laboratory studies of groups; rather, it is to provide the group member with a way of evaluating his own behavior and that of his peers. His new system is designed for the participant rather than the observer.

The three dimensions are called: (1) upward-downward (dominant versus submissive); (2) positive-negative; and (3) forward-backward (task-oriented and conforming versus deviant). Each of the original twelve categories in Bales' observational scheme can be used as a measure of some combination of the three dimensions. For example, a person who "shows solidarity" would be considered as acting in an upward and backward direction, or a person who "agrees" would be seen as acting in a positive and forward direction. Rather than translate from the twelve categories to the three dimensions, Bales has developed a twenty-six-term check list that can be used by group members to rate themselves or others and translate their ratings into a summary position in the three-dimensional space. After completing the ratings, the summary judgment may be checked against one of the twenty-six profiles that indicate behavior expected for persons with any given combination of the three dimensions. The three dimensions may also be used for the direct observation of behavior at several different system levels.

Nonverbal Behavior

Early research on interaction, that of Bales and others, usually included both verbal and nonverbal cues in the category systems developed for the classification of social interaction. More recently, some research has focused solely on the nonverbal aspects of behavior. Since nonverbal behavior may be less consciously controlled, it may contradict as well as amplify verbal behavior. Often research does not distinguish between nonverbal behaviors that a subject emits unconsciously, although they give information to others, and nonverbal signals that are consciously used in lieu of verbal communication or to supplement it.

The dimensions of nonverbal behavior are similar to those of verbal behavior. In some research the dimensions identified are clearly the same as those described earlier in this chapter; in others the authors present slightly different summations of traits! Albert Mehrabian, for example, identifies three dimensions: (1) evaluation, (2) potency or status, and (3) responsiveness. Increases in positive *evaluation* are denoted by immediate positions and postures (for example, a closer position, more forward lean, more eye contact, and more direct orientation); increases in *potency* or *status* are denoted by greater degrees of postural relaxation; and increases in *responsiveness* by greater activity—for example, facial activity, speech intonation, or speech rate.[66]

The principles of social exchange operate with nonverbal behavior as they do with verbal behavior. If an interviewer emits positive cues by facing the subject, leaning forward, maintaining eye contact, and smiling appropriately, then the subject will tend to respond by maintaining eye contact and smiling in return. If a subject seeks approval, the subject will offer smiles and positive head nods.

The forms of nonverbal behavior tend to be consistent over time for the same subject, but may vary across cultures. It has been suggested that behavior patterns such as smiling, nodding, and a very brief lift of the eyebrows particularly prominent in flirting behavior appear to be genetically fixed and are used in comparable situations of social contact in various cultures.

The amount of eye contact one person receives from another will affect the person's attitudes and emotional responses. Generally people look more at others they like, or from whom they seek approval. Women tend to look more and be more observant of eye contact than men.

As with other nonverbal behaviors, hand movements vary with personality. When persons are showing overt hostility, they tend to use large gestures that parallel their speech; when they are showing covert hostility, they engage in smaller, body-focused movements, such as playing with their fingers or clothing.

Voice is used to signal affection, as persons speak more often and for longer periods of time to those they prefer. In contrast, tension is reflected in longer pauses in speech. Although all persons tend to speak more loudly when they are farther away from other persons, males speak even more loudly than females.

Touching as a form of nonverbal behavior appears to be the privilege of high status as indicated by age, sex, race, or socioeconomic class. Persons of higher status tend to initiate touching. Touch also indicates intimacy and solidarity and may reduce stress in interpersonal relations.

The aims of this chapter have been to provide perspective on some major approaches to group social structure, to describe the different ways in which social structure has been conceived (as a network of affective relations, as a network of communication,

chapter eight

THE SOCIOLOGY OF SMALL GROUPS: COMMENTS AND PROPOSALS

This study is organized around three sets of distinctions: the distinction between the sociological and the psychological emphasis; between personality, culture, and social structure; and between primary-expressive and secondary-instrumental behavior. The fact that these distinctions do not derive from any particular "school" of small-group research—being, rather, in the public domain of social science—helps fix the discussion in a more general and less parochial framework than has customarily been the case in surveys of small-group research.

The familiarity of these distinctions contributes to—though, of course, it cannot insure—the study's achievement of the double aim announced in the Introduction. The newcomer is aided by having a frame of reference in terms of which to encounter the diversity of a new field; the more familiar the framework, the more useful it is likely to be. The professional also needs to maintain perspective amidst the day-to-day pressures of research; to this end, it is useful to see problems *sub specie aeternitatis*, as instances of more general processes or situations. The use of familiar distinctions may thus be seen as having potential positive advantages in promoting a broad and comparative perspective.

But any framework or descriptive procedure either distorts or fragments its subject matter—and the present one is no exception. Rather than try to ameliorate the distortion and fragmentation by *post facto* cautions and provisos, this chapter attempts a modicum of synthesis by means of two devices: a discussion of leadership, and the presentation of a synoptic model or paradigm for the analysis of group relationships.

LEADERSHIP

The study of leadership is in no way the special preserve of small-group analysts. Human beings have had ideas on this subject for as long—so we may suppose—as they have had ideas about any social principles. The qualities of good and bad leaders have been described at great length by philosophers, historians, political thinkers, prophets and, most recently, by research-minded social scientists. This latter effort, which is our present concern, received considerable impetus from World War I and from the growing self-consciousness of American business. Until the 1950s or so the voluminous writing on military and executive leadership dealt largely with leadership *traits:* intelligence, courage, independence, considerateness, decisiveness, and so on. For various reasons, most notably the lack of agreement on just which traits are the most important, the attention of investigators has in recent years shifted from the presumed traits of leaders to the *situations of leadership.*[1] The small group thereby became a useful context in which to study the phenomenon, or phenomena, of leadership.

In the study of small groups, the leadership "situation" has been conceived of both narrowly, as meaning group task or problem, and broadly, as referring to group functions or prerequisites of the problem-solving process. The former conception focuses attention on the differences and similarities of leadership as it is called forth by various tasks involving, say, mechanical skills or discussion skills or adaptiveness. The emphasis is on the external problem presented by the experimenter, and leadership is defined in terms of the efforts of group members to find solutions to this problem. The broader conception of "situation" takes into account the internal problems of group organization and the coordination of efforts, as well as the overt task given by the experimenter. It recognizes that various functions must be performed before the group can successfully cope with the external problem. Leadership, then, is defined in terms of the solution of a series of problems, only some of which are "instrumental" in the sense of accomplishing the task or adapting to the environment.

What are these group functions with reference to which leadership is to be defined? In their thoughtful review of this problem, Cartwright and Zander are unusually cautious: "It is not possible at the present stage of research on groups, to develop a fully satisfactory designation of the functions that are peculiarly functions of leadership. A more promising endeavor, at least for the present, is to identify the various group functions, without deciding finally whether or not to label each specifically as a function of leadership. ..."[2] These authors proceed to distinguish two basic types of group functions, those of *goal achievement* and those of *group maintenance*. This is our now-familiar distinction of task-oriented, instrumental, and guidance behavior, on the one hand, and group-oriented, expressive, and social behavior, on the other.

In addition to this task/group distinction, the literature on small groups reveals another way of conceiving of leadership functions, which may be referred to as the "fused" and the "segregated" conceptions of leader roles. In the former case, the leader performs many roles and fulfills many, if not all, of the group functions; in the latter, the appropriate behaviors are performed by many different individuals with the leader being restricted (or restricting himself) to one or two presumably crucial functions. The familiar distinctions between "directive" and "permissive" or between "leader-centered" and "group-centered" forms of leadership are instances of the fused/segregated distinction. It is in this vein that Homans describes leadership:

> The fact is that leadership in a group may be at one time abrupt, forceful, centralized, with all communications originating with

the leader, and at another time slow, relaxed, dispersed, with much communication back and forth between leader and followers. Each mode is acceptable, appropriate, and authoritative, but each in different circumstances.[3]

Helen Jennings, a sociometrist, likewise recognizes the diffuse or "segregated" character of leadership when she writes that leadership "appears as a process in which no one individual has a major role but in which relatively many share."[4]

There seems to be some tendency in discussions of leadership to associate "task" with "fused" conceptions and "social" with "segregated" conceptions. The former combination is represented by the driving taskmaster who wants to get things done, fast, and in his or her own way; the latter combination by the modest, sociable, "democratic" type whose first concern is group morale. Furthermore, there has been a tendency to assume that the latter style of leadership is not only more satisfactory to members but more productive as well. Considerable evidence supports this generalization, but there is also evidence indicating its limitations. Thus, a study of seventy-two conference groups in business and government found that group members liked leaders who stressed direction: "the more the chairman is the sole major behavioral leader the more satisfied the group is with its conference."[5] Another investigation found that the satisfaction of conferees was positively related to the degree of procedural control by the leader.[6] A study of permissive and directive teaching methods concluded that students in both types of classes preferred to have more rather than less directive teaching.[7] Yet none of this research provides an adequate basis (nor was it designed to do so) for reversing the preference cited above for democratic-permissive group procedures. Either because the research was limited to special types of group situations or because other findings in the same investigations underlined the advantages of permissiveness, the results do not add up to advocacy of "strong" methods of leadership. They add perceptibly, however, to one's common-sense objections to the rather uncritical acceptance of unalloyed permissiveness—an acceptance which, emerging partly because of and partly despite the Lippitt and White studies, reflects the utopian strain in much small-group research.

If, as has been argued, the task versus social conceptions of leadership on the one hand and the fused versus segregated conceptions on the other represent differences, then other combinations are possible—specifically the "fused-social" and the "segregated-task" types of leadership. An example of the former is the "charismatic" group dominated by a single compelling personality. Such groups are common enough in history but are not easily reproduced in the laboratory. The "segregated-task" type of group organization is illustrated by a string quartet: leadership functions are diffused and at the same time devoted to task accomplishment rather than to interpersonal solidarity.

These four types do not exhaust the possible forms of leadership one may find in small groups. This is partly because any typology is essentially a device for simplifying empirical richness and variation, and partly because it is not even as adequate a typology as can be derived from the full use of the dimensions described in this study. The introduction of a few other already familiar distinctions produces a typology that is more complex and also more suggestive of the *processes* as well as the *forms* of group organization and leadership. Rather than continuing to emphasize "leadership," it is possible—and, for the student of small groups, advantageous—to refocus on the concept of group organization. In this perspective, leadership can be treated as a special case of the more general phenomenon of role differentiation.

A PARADIGM FOR GROUP ANALYSIS

By drawing together the major dimensions of analysis employed in this study, we can construct a model or paradigm that should prove useful in understanding the dynamics of groups and the processes of leadership which reflect them. This needs to be done, even at the risk of being abstruse, for authors must make explicit the basis from which they evaluate the contributions of others.

The distinctions to be employed are those between (1) culture and social structure, (2) instrumental and expressive activity, and (3) the processes of differentiation and integration. These are combined in Figure 5, which presents in synoptic form many of the ideas found on earlier pages. Like all paradigms, this one represents a rather abstract view of things and tends to split up and recombine elements in a way that may run counter to some of our common-sense impressions. The most obvious instance of this splitting up is the paradigm's delineation of a number of types of "leader roles." We have already seen how investigators have called into question the frequent assumption that every group has *a* leader; this paradigm spells out that critical view.

It will be observed that within each of the four major numbered cells in the diagram, a further distinction is made—signified by the letters a and b. This distinction, which inheres in any system made up of parts, is between the processes of differentiation and integration. A *system*, as distinguished from what we might call an entity, consists of parts that are in some way different from one another in nature or function; these parts must be coordinated if the system is to maintain itself as a system rather than as a collection or congeries. We may think of differentiation as a centrifugal and integration as a centripetal process. Differentiation, moreover, is associated with the specialization of parts (or specialized roles, in the small-group context) and integration with generalization (or generalized roles).

The most familiar case of differentiation and integration is that of instrumental activity relative to social structure (cell 2 in Figure 5): on the one hand, there is the specialization of roles which on the charts of bureaucratic or formal organizations is represented by the little boxes labeled "Production Department," "Accounting," "Sales," and so forth. On the other hand, there is the structure of authority, the hierarchical arrangement of offices which in the bureaucratic blueprint is represented by the "line organization" (as distinguished from the specialized or "staff organization") and includes such personnel as the general manager, the executive secretary, and so forth. This distinction, here

	Culture ("Outer" situation—relationships among ideas and values)	Social structure ("Inner" situation—relationships among members)
Instrumental Activity	(1) Adaptation *Dimension of cultural symbols:* Knowledge, information *Leader roles:* (a) idea man, analyst (b) synthesizer	(2) Goal attainment *Dimension of social activity:* (a) the division of labor—staff functions (b) the structure of authority—line or guidance functions *Leader roles:* (a) technical expert (b) executive
Expressive Activity	(4) Latent pattern maintenance and tension management *Dimension of cultural symbols:* Values *Leader roles:* (a) style setter, artist (b) symbolic figurehead, consensus creator ("the crown")	(3) Integration *Dimension of social activity:* (a) network of affective ties (b) solidarity *Leader roles:* (a) best liked (b) harmonizer (host role)

FIGURE 5.   Paradigm of Group Dimensions

labeled as (a) and (b) dimensions and roles, is one of long standing in most large-scale formal organizations.

Is there any reason to suppose that the distinction between (a) differentiation-specialization and (b) integration-generalization is *not* applicable to the other areas of the paradigm? It seems possible, in cell 1, to distinguish the role of the analyst (a) and that of the synthesizer (b): in actual groups one often encounters a member with a flow of original ideas and another member who is adept at putting together the contributions of others. It may be that one individual performs both roles, but in theory at least, they are different functions. In a discussion group, where the only things people work with are symbols or words, the dimensions of social activity (2) and of cultural symbols (1) are very much the same. In larger societies, however, we find the distinction between "doers" (for example, persons engaged in business) and "thinkers" (for example, academics) given rather more than sufficient recognition.

In the realm of what is here called expressive activity (cells 3 and 4), similar distinctions can be made. With reference to the relationships among members, we may recognize, on the one hand, the differentiating tendencies of "personal" affective bonds and animosities that, unless controlled, are likely to have a centrifugal effect, and on the other hand, the centripetal processes that unite the parts into a solidary whole. (This is essentially what Freud referred to when he argued that it was necessary that the separate "object choices" be converted into common identifications.[8]) The role types that follow from this distinction are not customarily specified (perhaps because in the small group the two roles tend, for reasons which are as yet unclear, to be united in the same individual). Proceeding deductively, however, we may hypothesize the specialized "best-liked" role and the generalized "harmonizer" role, whose incumbent sees to it, as it were, that loves and hates do not get out of hand. The role of "host," for example, is one whose incumbent is not necessarily tops in popularity, but which may be said to perform important affective functions nonetheless. On the negative affective side, there is the problem of controlling the resentments and hostilities that are likely to exist both by virtue of personality conflicts and by virtue of the friction generated in the course of arriving at group decisions. Among the integrating processes useful for dealing with these difficulties are repression and projection. The former may be assisted by the presence of what Redl calls the "good example," the individual who provides a model of an unconflicted (that is, well-repressed) personality; the latter by a scapegoat or by someone who—by jokes, righteous indignation, or other means—turns the hostile impulses outward to external objects.* It seems reasonable to suppose that none of these roles need necessarily be held by the member whom other members choose as the best liked or the most fun to be with.

In cell 4, finally, we may place values about the good and the beautiful. The specialized differentiating role here is represented by the taste-maker, the definer of prestigeful living, and the artist, who refines old values into new ones. The more generalized integrating role is that of the figurehead who, rather than *doing* something, *stands for* something—namely, the moral consensus of the group. This symbolic role, as noted many years ago by Emile Durkheim and Georg Simmel, can be held either by an individual or by an abstract principle such as the crown, the flag, or the tribal totem.[9] These individuals, or principles, serve to legitimize the normative (value) structure and the social organization of the group.[10]

Considering this paradigm with relation to the previous discussion of leadership, it seems that the task-group distinction is essentially one of emphasis upon activity in cell 1 and secondarily cell 2, as over against cell 3. The permissive-directive dichotomy appears to be the contrast between the combination of "leader roles" 1b–2b–3b on the one hand and of "leader roles" 1a–1b–2a–2b on the other. In other words, while the directive leaders take all the group business under their wings, the permissive leaders do not try to solve but only to resolve; they do not drive others to their solutions but coordinate the ideas and mollify the feelings of their companions. Stated more generally, permissive leadership is one type of relatively "segregated" leadership, while directive leadership is relatively "fused," embracing more of the instrumental functions to the neglect of expressive-affective functions. These equations or definitions of leadership roles in terms of the paradigm are necessarily tentative, in part because

*The philosopher Friedrich Nietzsche, who was never one to overlook a psychic impulse, gave great prominence to this role in his analysis of society. He saw a certain type of intellectual ideologist (to whom he gave the name "ascetic priest") as partly responsible for social cohesion: "Getting rid of the blasting-stuff [resentment] in such a way that it does not blow up the herd and the herdsman, that is his [the ascetic priest's] real feat, his supreme utility.... The priest is the diverter of the course of resentment." *The Genealogy of Morals,* in *The Philosophy of Nietzsche* (New York: Modern Library), p. 753.

the commonly used conceptions vary in the emphasis they assign to the roles distinguished in the theoretical paradigm. It seems fair to say that both the "fused" and the "segregated" conceptions of leadership involve a *combination* of roles as they are defined here; the former is only a different and more extensive combination than the latter.[11]

The paradigm for group dimensions can be used to identify types of follower roles as well as types of leader roles. Since followers must join with leaders to solve the system problems faced by any group, it is not surprising that the analysis of follower behavior yields a set of roles similar to those of leaders. In general, the person who initiates most of the activity in a given area is seen as the leader, while the person who reacts to these initiations is seen as the follower. Although many category systems have been used to observe member behavior, the resulting set of dimensions is usually similar to the three identified by Bales, except that his third dimension can be split in two, giving four major dimensions of interpersonal behavior: (1) dominant versus submissive; (2) positive versus negative; (3) serious versus expressive; (4) conforming versus nonconforming.[12]

If we assume that behavior at the extremes of each dimension may identify a member role, then we find a rather good fit between the extremes of the first three dimensions and six role patterns identified by Jerry Cloyd without reference to any particular dimensions and without actually assigning them names.[13] At the dominance end of the first dimension we find a set of behaviors that includes "aggressive, self-confident, and gets things started." This role might be called the "high talker." At the submissive end of the first dimension is the cluster of traits "modest, shy, and ill at ease." This role might be called the "silent member." In a similar way one can identify a "supporter," who is friendly and objective, a "critic," who is idealistic and argumentative, a "serious worker," who is dependable and constructive, and a "joker," who makes humorous remarks and challenges the opinions of others. Cloyd does not provide examples that would fit the ends of the fourth dimension; the last dimension, however, suggests the roles of "conformist" and "nonconformist."

These four dimensions of interaction which are represented

by eight member roles are in turn related to the four cells in the paradigm of group dimensions. The roles of high talker and silent member are primarily related to cell 2, supporter and critic to cell 3, serious worker and joker to cell 1, and conformist and nonconformist to cell 4.

Underlying this paradigm are the assumptions of functional prerequisites and of equilibrium in social systems. The first assumption holds that there are certain problems, such as evaluation and coordination, that have to be solved if the system is to be maintained; the second assumption embodies the notion that a group's activity devoted to these problems must be kept in some kind of balance. This does not mean perfect, and certainly not self-conscious, balance, but only that some activity is devoted to the various problems from time to time. Equilibrium is thus both a temporal (distributed through time) and a structural (distributed among persons) phenomenon. Indeed, equilibrium is implicit in the concept of system itself. To be accurate, we should speak of equilibria, for there are more ways than one in which a group may go about its business and still hang together. The function of a paradigm is to suggest possible alternative types of equilibria, and more broadly, to set forth in systematic fashion the possible forms and categories of group organization. A paradigm, furthermore, should serve as a framework within which it is possible to "locate" various pieces of research and various approaches to one's subject matter. Whether the present paradigm performs all these services to the satisfaction of all students of small groups must remain an open question. At a minimum, however, it summarizes and organizes the major themes that have been developed in these pages.

Both the paradigm of group dimensions and Jahoda's types of pressures toward attitude change (discussed in Chapter 5) are congruent with the "Four Functions" or AGIL scheme for the analysis of groups developed in large part by Talcott Parsons and his colleagues to provide a comprehensive theory for the study of groups.[14] The four categories of the AGIL scheme—adaptation (A), goal attainment (G), integration (I), and latent (L) pattern maintenance and tension management (or simply pattern maintenance)—were derived empirically from an analysis of small groups, psychotherapy, and the economic factors in production. The basic assumption is that all groups, whether small discussion groups or total societies, must meet four basic needs if they are to survive: (L) the members must share some common identity and have some commitment to the values of the group; (A) they must be able to generate the skills and resources necessary to reach the group goal; (I) they must have rules that allow them to coordinate their activity and enough feeling of solidarity to stay together to complete the task; and finally (G) they must be able to exercise enough control over their membership to be effective in reaching their common goal.

The cells in the paradigm for group dimensions are arranged to show the theoretical relationship between the four functions. Cell 1 represents the function of adaptation, cell 2 of goal attainment, cell 3 of integration, and cell 4 of latent pattern maintenance and tension management. The four processes of conformism used in Jahoda's analysis also fit the AGIL scheme directly if we rotate Figure 2 (see p. 71) counterclockwise one cell: the process of convergence is related to adaptation (A), since it is based on facts; compliance to goal attainment (G), since it is based on the power of authority; conformance to integration (I), since it is based on friendship ties; and consentience to pattern maintenance (L), since it is based on adherence to basic values.

GROUP DEVELOPMENT

Small groups and other social systems up to and including whole societies seem to develop through a sequence of stages in the order L–A–I–G.[15] In a learning group, as in a classroom, the sequence of events seems to be as follows: first, the work of the group requires that the purpose of the group be defined (L); second, that new skills be acquired (A); third, that the group be reorganized so that the members can try out the new skills without being too dependent on the leader (I); and fourth, that the group members work at the task (G). Finally there is a terminal phase in which the group returns to L to redefine the relationships between the members and the group as a group is disbanded. The amount of time the group spends in each phase is determined by the activity of the leader (the leader's direction or nondirection) and by the skills and emotional strengths of the members. Presumably the leader is ready for each stage at the outset, since the leader/teacher has been through the stages before. However, members come to the group with different degrees of problem-solving skill or preferences for different emotional modalities. If the subgroup with the appropriate skills and emotional state for each stage is large enough, it can carry the whole group through that phase. If not enough members of the group are ready for a particular stage, more intervention by the leader may be necessary. Some groups may never progress beyond the early stages.

What seems to be happening is that the members of a group "test the limits" in the different functional areas as they try to determine whether or not they can form a fully functioning group. It is not difficult to see that a group must begin with a basic purpose (L) and end with the enactment of that purpose (G), but whether A should come before I or vice versa may not be immediately clear. The dramatic example of a trip to the moon might help. Once there is the idea of the possibility of the trip (L), one can imagine different types of group organization (I) that would be effective. However, these plans are limited by the availability of a rocket big enough to lift a group to the moon. If only a small rocket is available, the effort becomes an individual task rather than a group task. If it is to be a group task, the presence of two, three, or more astronauts is again determined by the size of the rocket. Thus, although the rocket represents the raw energy and is in general controlled by the other parts of the social system, there can be no movement without it. In this case, moreover, and in general, the availability and complexity of equipment may determine whether or not a single individual can achieve the goal or whether a group is required. Once resources are assured, the group can go on to define the roles of the group members and develop group morale (I) before proceeding to carry out the actual work of the group (G).

CONCLUDING REMARKS

The study of small groups has both its practical and its theoretical rationale. It is useful for finding out how to improve meetings and conferences; and it aids in our understanding of how people interrelate with one another. The practical rationale calls for no comment here other than that it is probably the dominant motive for small-group research today; in this respect it reflects the pragmatic tendencies of American social science and of American society. The theoretical rationale, in which sheer curiosity may be said to play a chief role, deserves a final word.

That people manage to cooperate is obvious. It is so obvious, in fact, that we are disposed to think of it as "natural"—that is, as being in the nature of things and not requiring any particular explanation—until something goes wrong. When we reflect on the matter at all, we are likely to echo Aristotle and say that "man is by nature a political [that is, social] animal." In a general way this is true enough, but to find the explanation of social interaction in a characteristic of the individual obliterates the distinction between sociology and psychology and thereby obscures the very phenomena which require clarification. The argument here, then, is that group life remains problematic even when it seems most "natural" and most trouble-free.

Small-group research, for all its attention to problem-solving groups, does not yet treat its subject matter as sufficiently problematic in the above sense. It tends to be distinguished more by its technological enthusiasms than by its fondness for sessions of sweet silent thought. These shortcomings are in good part those of the newer social sciences generally, with their predilections for cleverness and immediately perceptible problems.

In addition, it may be ventured that the limited success of small-group research owes something to its common, though by no means universal, tendency to be concerned with individuals rather than with roles. To be sure, the group is made up of individuals, and group behavior is a compound of individual behaviors. But it is also a compound of social roles, of sets of expectations and of articulated functions that ought to be conceived of sociologically as well as psychologically. If one takes seriously the familiar sociological contention that society is a reality *sui generis* and is not simply the individual writ large, then society must be conceived as some set of institutions or some system of roles, and not merely as a plurality of individuals. It may be argued, of course, that the sociologist, like everybody else, "sees" only individuals* and does not in any direct sense perceive patterns of social structure or of culture. The latter are inferred, rather than perceived, but this does not make them any less useful to the would-be analyst. The situation here is analogous to that in physics where the scientist does not perceive directly but only infers the existence of mass and velocity from falling weights and rolling balls.

The predominance of psychologists in small-group research is probably responsible for much of the emphasis on individuals and the neglect of roles and their articulation in social structures. This individualist emphasis has not been unproductive, but it does seem that hitherto relatively unexplored paths may yield returns at least as great as those promised by further elaboration of established techniques. For their part, sociologists may have something to gain from an increased concern with sophisticated analyses of small groups. In small compass, they can find many, although not all, of the properties of social systems: stratification, role differentiation, mechanisms of social control, and the like.

The "will to truth," which science most systematically embodies, opens up for us—whether we like it or not—the yawning chasm beneath our feet; it reveals that the world is more problematic than we had supposed. The social sciences have had their share in this, perhaps most notably exemplified in the work of Freud, who dramatized the intricacy and uncertainty of all personality formation. Small-group research can perhaps find here another *raison d'etre:* it may be able to generate the habit of seeing inner complexities, and in so doing, it may help us to discern the submerged foundations on which truly social behavior rests. Granted, these insights do not come only from the study of small groups. Still, the small group is a convenient locus wherein to assay one of the individual's more baffling qualities— the ability to get along with one's fellow creatures.

*Actually, the sociologist does not see individuals but organisms. The concept of "the individual" or even further, of "the personality," as we have seen, is an abstraction in the same sense as are the concepts of culture and social structure.

NOTES

chapter one

1. Josephine Klein, *The Study of Groups* (New York: Humanities Press, 1956). Henry W. Riecken and George C. Homans, "Psychological Aspects of Social Structure," *Handbook of Social Psychology*, 1st ed., Gardner Lindzey (Cambridge: Addison-Wesley, 1954), vol. 2.
2. Robert E. L. Faris, "Development of the Small-Group Research Movement," *Group Relations at the Crossroads*, ed. Muzafer Sherif and M. O. Wilson (New York: Harper, 1953); Logan Wilson, "The Sociography of Groups," *Twentieth-Century Sociology*, ed. Georges Gurvitch and Wilbert Moore (New York: Philosophical Library, 1945); Edward A. Shils, "The Study of the Primary Group," *The Policy Sciences*, ed. Daniel Lerner and Harold Lasswell, Hoover Institute Series (Stanford: Stanford University Press, 1951).

chapter two

1. For a survey of such typologies, see Logan Wilson, "Sociography of Groups," pp. 134–171.
2. Charles H. Cooley, *Social Organization* (New York: Charles Scribner, 1909), pp. 23–24, 26–28.

3. Albion W. Small, *General Sociology* (Chicago: University of Chicago Press, 1905), p. 495.

chapter three

1. See Fritz J. Roethlisberger and William J. Dickson, *Management and the Worker* (Cambridge: Harvard University Press, 1947).
2. See, for instance, Donald G. Marquis, Harold Guetzkow, and Roger W. Heyns, "A Social Psychological Study of the Decision-Making Conference," *Groups, Leadership and Men*, ed. Harold Guetzkow (Pittsburgh: Carnegie Press, 1951).
3. Frederic M. Thrasher, *The Gang* (Chicago: University of Chicago Press, 1927), pp. 288, 295n. It will be noted that Thrasher does not assume that primary-group relations are inevitably solidary, affective, or nonlogical.
4. Ibid., p. 328.
5. Ibid., p. 326.
6. Ibid., pp. 345–352.
7. Ibid., p. 353.
8. Ibid., pp. 289–297.
9. William F. Whyte, *Street Corner Society* (Chicago: University of Chicago Press, 1943).
10. See Whyte's diagram on p. 13, ibid.
11. Ibid., pp. 258–261.
12. Ibid., pp. 259–260.
13. Ibid., p. 58.
14. For theoretically sophisticated treatments of many of these problems, see Albert K. Cohen, *Delinquent Boys: The Culture of the Gang* (Glencoe, Ill.: Free Press, 1955), and Lewis Yablonsky, *The Violent Gang* (New York: Macmillan, 1962).
15. For the most convenient summary of this research, see Ronald Lippitt and Ralph K. White, "An Experimental Study of Leadership and Group Life," *Readings in Social Psychology*, 3rd ed., ed. Eleanor E. Maccoby, Theodore M. Newcomb, and Eugene L. Hartley (New York: Holt, Rinehart and Winston, 1958).
16. Ibid., p. 496.
17. Ibid., p. 498.
18. Ibid., p. 504.
19. Ibid., pp. 503–504.
20. Ibid., p. 505.
21. Ibid., p. 510.
22. Theodore M. Newcomb, *The Acquaintance Process* (New York: Holt, Rinehart and Winston, 1961), and also by the same author, "Stabilities Underlying Changes in Interpersonal Attraction," *Journal of Abnormal and Social Psychology* 66, 4 (April 1963).

23. Samuel A. Stouffer et al., *The American Soldier: Studies in Social Psychology in World War II* (Princeton: Princeton University Press, 1949).
24. Edward A. Shils, "Primary Groups in the American Army," *Continuities in Social Research: Studies in the Scope and Method of "The American Soldier,"* ed. Robert Merton and Paul Lazarsfeld (Glencoe, Ill.: Free Press, 1950).
25. Quoted in ibid., p. 25.
26. Ibid., p. 22.
27. See Roy R. Grinker and John P. Spiegel, *Men Under Stress* (Philadelphia: Blakiston, 1945), especially chaps. 2 and 3. Also Edward A. Shils and Morris Janowitz, "Cohesion and Disintegration in the Wehrmacht in World War II," *Public Opinion Quarterly* 12 (1948).
28. Elihu Katz and Paul F. Lazarsfeld, *Personal Influence: The Part Played by People in the Flow of Mass Communication* (Glencoe, Ill.: Free Press, 1955), pp. 19–20.
29. Ibid., p. 131.
30. Ibid., pp. 41–42.

chapter four

1. Cf. George Herbert Mead, *Mind, Self and Society* (Chicago: University of Chicago Press, 1934).
2. Emile Durkheim, *The Division of Labor in Society* (Glencoe, Ill.: Free Press, 1947). Preface to the second edition, p. 15. Copyright 1933 by the Macmillan Company.
3. See Peter M. Blau and Marshall W. Meyer, *Bureaucracy in Modern Society,* 2nd ed. (New York: Random House, 1971).
4. See Max Weber, *The Theory of Social and Economic Organization,* ed. Talcott Parsons (New York: Oxford University Press, 1947), pt. 1. Also Ernst Troeltsch, *The Social Teachings of the Christian Churches,* 2 vols., trans. Olive Wyon (London: George Allen & Unwin, 1950).
5. Alexis de Tocqueville, *Democracy in America* (Galaxy ed.), trans. Henry Reeve, ed. Henry Steele Commager (New York: Oxford University Press, 1947), p. 319. The greatest sociologist of modern times, Max Weber, made similar observations upon his trip to the United States in 1904. His particular interest was in the role played by the sect form of organization in American Protestantism and society generally. Cf. "The Protestant Sects and the Spirit of Capitalism," *From Max Weber: Essays in Sociology,* ed. Hans H. Gerth and C. Wright Mills (New York: Oxford University Press, 1946).

6. Tocqueville, *Democracy in America*, p. 323.
7. Jean Jacques Rousseau, *The Social Contract*, bk. 2, chap. 3.
8. Durkheim, *Division of Labor*, pp. 28–29. It is interesting that Durkheim, who so resolutely opposes Rousseau on this point, apparently owes much of his conception of the moral nature of society to Rousseau's *The Social Contract.*
9. See, for instance, among the sophisticated sociological treatments: Philip Selznick, *The Organizational Weapon* (New York: McGraw-Hill, 1952), chap. 7; Hannah Arendt, *The Origins of Totalitarianism* (New York: Harcourt, 1951), pt. 3; Carl J. Friedrich, ed., *Totalitarianism* (Cambridge: Harvard University Press, 1954). An earlier work which has influenced these authors is Erich Fromm's *Escape From Freedom* (New York: Farrar & Rinehart, 1941).
10. Robert Nisbet, *The Quest for Community* (New York: Oxford University Press, 1953), p. 47.
11. Ibid., p. 49.
12. Ibid., p. 52.
13. Ibid., p. 31.
14. Edward A. Shils, "Primordial, Personal, Sacred and Civil Ties," *British Journal of Sociology* 8 (June 1957).
15. Cf. Robert J. Lifton, *Thought Reform and the Psychology of Totalism: A Study of "Brainwashing" in China* (New York: Norton, 1961), and Edgar H. Schein, Inge Schneier, and Curtis H. Barker, *Coercive Persuasion* (New York: Norton, 1961).
16. Ernest Burgess and Harvey Locke, *The Family, From Institution to Companionship* (New York: American Book, 1945).
17. Cf. Carl J. Friedrich and Zbigniew Brzezinski, *Totalitarian Dictatorship and Autocracy* (Cambridge: Harvard University Press, 1956).
18. For a brilliant essay on this theme, see Eric Hoffer, *The True Believer* (New York: Harper, 1951). For supporting data, see Gabriel Almond, *The Appeals of Communism* (Princeton: Princeton University Press, 1954).
19. Cf. Kurt W. Back, *Beyond Words* (Baltimore: Penguin Books, 1973); Rosabeth Moss Kanter, ed., *Communes: Creating and Managing the Collective Life* (New York: Harper, 1973); and Theodore Roszak, *The Making of a Counter Culture: Reflections on the Technocratic Society and Its Youthful Opposition* (London: Faber & Faber, 1970). For more information about sensitivity training, see also Cary L. Cooper, "How Psychologically Dangerous Are T-groups and Encounter Groups?" *Human Relations* 28, 3 (April 1975); J. William Pfeiffer and John E. Jones, eds., *Structured Experiences of Human Relations Training: A Reference Guide* (Iowa City: University Associates, 1974); and Peter B. Smith, "Controlled Studies of the Outcome of Sensitivity Training," *Psychological Bulletin* 82, 4 (July

1975). Most of the groups involved in communes and sensitivity training included both men and women.

chapter five

1. Harold H. Kelley and John W. Thibaut, "Experimental Studies of Group Problem Solving and Process," *Handbook of Social Psychology*, 1st ed., vol. 2, p. 750.
2. Allport felt that the facilitating effects were far more important than the distracting ones. See the summary of his research in Floyd Allport, "The Influence of the Group upon Association and Thought," *Small Groups*, 2nd ed., ed. A. Paul Hare, Edgar F. Borgatta, and Robert F. Bales (New York: Knopf, 1965), p. 34.
3. Peter J. Hunt and Joseph M. Hillery, "Social Facilitation in a Coaction Setting: An Examination of the Effects of Learning Over Trials," *Journal of Experimental Social Psychology* 9 (November 1973). See also Robert B. Zajonc, "Social Facilitation," *Science* 149 (1965).
4. Kurt Lewin, "Group Decision and Social Change," *Readings in Social Psychology*, 3rd ed., p. 210.
5. Kelley and Thibaut, "Experimental Studies . . . ," p. 757.
6. Muzafer Sherif, "Group Influences upon the Formation of Norms and Attitudes," *Readings in Social Psychology*, 3rd ed., pp. 219–232. It will be noted that this study is akin to the standard psychological investigation of prestige and suggestibility but that in this instance there is no special source of influence set up either by the subjects or by the experimenter to which superior qualifications or prestige are ascribed.
7. Solomon E. Asch, "Effects of Group Pressure upon the Modification and Distortion of Judgments," *Readings in Social Psychology*, 3rd ed., pp. 178–179.
8. Ibid., p. 182.
9. Marie Jahoda, "Psychological Issues in Civil Liberties," *American Psychologist* 11 (1956), pp. 236, 237.
10. See Robert K. Merton and Alice Kitt, "Contributions to the Theory of Reference Group Behavior," *Continuities in Social Research*, pp. 40–105.
11. Max Rosenbaum and Alvin Snadowsky, eds., *The Intensive Group Experience* (New York: Free Press, 1976).
12. Irvin D. Yalom, *The Theory and Practice of Group Psychotherapy* (New York: Basic Books, 1970), p. 5.
13. Samuel R. Slavson, *Analytic Group Psychotherapy with Children, Adolescents and Adults* (New York: Columbia University Press, 1950), p. 10.

14. A happy exception to this generalization is provided by the ruminations of the English psychiatrist W. R. Bion, who in a series of articles collected in a book has attempted to create the rudiments of a theory of group culture and group social structure suitable for psychotherapy. W. R. Bion, *Experiences in Groups* (New York: Basic Books, 1961).

15. Even in such a relatively sophisticated book as Florence Powdermaker and Jerome Frank, *Group Psychotherapy: Studies in Methodology of Research and Therapy* (Cambridge: Harvard University Press, 1953).

16. Robert C. Ziller, "Four Techniques of Group Decision Making under Uncertainty," *Journal of Applied Psychology* 41 (1957).

17. James A. F. Stoner, "A Comparison of Individual and Group Decisions Involving Risk" (M.S. thesis, Massachusetts Institute of Technology, 1961).

18. Michael A. Wallach, Nathan Kogan, and Daryl J. Bem, "Group Influence on Individual Risk Taking," *Journal of Abnormal and Social Psychology* 65, 2 (August 1962).

19. For references to the research literature see pp. 326–329 in A. Paul Hare, *Handbook of Small Group Research* (New York: Free Press, 1976).

chapter six

1. Durkheim, *The Division of Labor in Society,* p. 14.

2. Kelley and Thibaut, "Experimental Studies . . . ," p. 738ff. See also Mary E. Roseborough, "Experimental Studies of Small Groups," *Psychological Bulletin* 50 (1953), pp. 276–277.

3. Examples of research include the following: Bertram Schoner, Gerald L. Rose, and G. C. Hoyt, "Quality of Decisions: Individuals Versus Real and Synthetic Groups," *Journal of Applied Psychology* 59, 4 (1974); William M. Wiest, Lyman W. Porter, and Edwin E. Ghiselli, "Relationship Between Individual Proficiency and Team Performance and Efficiency," *Journal of Applied Psychology* 45, 6 (1961); Patrick R. Laughlin and Laurence G. Branch, "Individual Versus Tetradic Performance on a Complementary Task as a Function of Initial Ability Level," *Organizational Behavior and Human Performance* 8, 2 (October 1972); and Salvatore V. Zagona, Joe E. Willis, and William J. MacKinnon, "Group Effectiveness in Creative Problem-Solving Tasks: An Examination of Relevant Variables," *Journal of Psychology* 62, 1 (1966).

4. Kelley and Thibaut, "Experimental Studies . . . ," p. 755. See also Chapter 5 of this study.

5. For examples of research, see Thomas J. Bouchard, Jr., Gail

Drauden, and Jean Barsaloux, "A Comparison of Individual, Sub-group, and Total Group Methods of Problem Solving," *Journal of Applied Psychology* 59, 2 (1974); Warren R. Street, "Brainstorming by Individuals, Coacting and Interacting Groups," *Journal of Applied Psychology* 59, 4 (1974); William K. Graham and Peter C. Dillon, "Creative Supergroups: Group Performance as a Function of Individual Performance on Brainstorming Tasks," *Journal of Social Psychology* 93, 1 (1974); Helmut Lamm and Gisela Tromms-dorff, "Group Versus Individual Performance on Tasks Requiring Ideational Proficiency (Brainstorming): A Review," *European Journal of Social Psychology* 3, 4 (1973); and Morris I. Stein, *Stimulating Creativity: II. Group Procedures* (New York: Academic Press, 1975).

6. For an example of research on decision rules, see J. David Edelstein and Malcolm Warner, "Voting and Allied Systems in Group Decision-Making: Their Relationship to Innovation, Competition and Conflict Resolution," *Human Relations* 24, 2 (1971).

7. See Eugen Kogon, *The Theory and Practice of Hell* (New York: Farrar, Straus, n.d.).

8. Kelley and Thibaut, "Experimental Studies . . . ," p. 754.

9. In a study by Beatrice Shriver it was found that experimental group leaders rebelled when asked to reward their fellow members differentially, in this case by paying them different amounts for their contributions to group problem-solving. They felt that to do so would be to violate deep-seated norms of group solidarity. This research is cited in Launor F. Carter, "Leadership and Small Group Behavior," *Group Relations at the Crossroads*, p. 280.

10. Cf. Peter M. Blau, *The Dynamics of Bureaucracy* (Chicago: University of Chicago Press, 1955).

11. Michael S. Olmsted, "Orientation and Role in the Small Group," *American Sociological Review* 19, 6 (December 1954).

chapter seven

1. Efforts in the direction of the encyclopedic inventory are represented by the chapters by Deutsch, by Kelley and Thibaut, and by Riecken and Homans in *Handbook of Social Psychology*, 1st ed. See also Josephine Klein, *The Study of Groups;* Mary E. Roseborough, "Experimental Studies of Small Groups."

2. See Renato Tagiuri, "Relational Analysis," *Sociometry* 15 (1952); Matilda W. Riley, John Riley, Jr., and Jackson Toby, *Sociological Studies in Scale Analysis* (New Brunswick: Rutgers University Press, 1954); and J. L. Moreno, ed., *The Sociometry Reader* (New York: Free Press, 1960).

3. See Helen H. Jennings, "The Sociometric Differentiation of the Psychegroup and the Sociogroup," *Sociometry* 10 (1947). The major research of both Jennings and Moreno on sociometric groupings was done at a training school for delinquent girls at Hudson, New York. Most of the sociometric research that followed was conducted in elementary and high schools in regular classes of boys and girls. Often the purpose of giving the sociometric tests was to place groups of friends together to provide a more effective setting for classwork.

4. Edward A. Shils, "The Study of the Primary Group," pp. 44–69.

5. Most people using the sociometric method to study leadership apparently overlooked the fact that Moreno had made it clear that the leader was not necessarily the person with the most choices. Rather, the leader was the one who received the most choices from the powerful members of the group. See J. L. Moreno, *Who Shall Survive?* rev. ed. (Beacon, N.Y.: Beacon House, 1953), p. 707.

6. Sigmund Freud, *Group Psychology and the Analysis of the Ego,* International Psychoanalytic Library (London: Hogarth Press, 1948), p. 80.

7. Fritz Redl, "Group Emotion and Leadership," *Psychiatry* 5, 4 (1942), pp. 573–596. See also Saul Scheidlinger, *Psychoanalysis and Group Behavior: A Study of Freudian Group Psychology* (New York: Norton, 1952).

8. Alex Bavelas, "Communication Patterns in Task-Oriented Groups," *Group Dynamics,* 3rd ed., ed. Dorwin Cartwright and Alvin Zander (Evanston, Ill.: Row, Peterson, 1968), pp. 503–511.

9. Harold J. Leavitt, "Some Effects of Certain Communication Patterns on Group Performance," *Readings in Social Psychology,* 3rd ed., p. 558.

10. Marvin E. Shaw, "A Comparison of Two Types of Leadership in Various Communication Nets," *Journal of Abnormal and Social Psychology* 50 (1955).

11. A. Paul Hare, "Cultural Differences in Performance in Communication Networks in Africa, the United States, and the Philippines," *Sociology and Social Research* 54, 1 (1969).

12. References to the literature on seating position and personal space are given in A. Paul Hare, *Handbook of Small Group Research,* pp. 275–276. See also Julian J. Edney, "Human Territoriality," *Psychological Bulletin* 81, 12 (December 1974).

13. George C. Homans, *The Human Group* (New York: Harcourt, 1950). With permission of the author and publisher.

14. Ibid., p. 90.

15. Ibid., pp. 109–110.

16. Riecken and Homans, "Psychological Aspects of Social Structure," *Handbook of Social Psychology,* 1st ed., vol. 2.

17. Homans, *The Human Group*, p. 133.
18. Ibid., p. 135.
19. Riecken and Homans, "Psychological Aspects of Social Structure," p. 791.
20. Ibid., p. 795.
21. Homans, *The Human Group*, p. 184.
22. Riecken and Homans, "Psychological Aspects of Social Structure," p. 818.
23. Homans, *The Human Group*, p. 445.
24. For instance, in *Group Dynamics*, 3rd ed., and *Handbook of Social Psychology*, 1st ed.
25. For an overview of work done by this group, see *Institute for Social Research, 1946–1956*, University of Michigan, Ann Arbor.
26. Morton Deutsch, "Field Theory in Social Psychology," *Handbook of Social Psychology*, 1st ed., vol. 1, pp. 182–185.
27. Kurt Lewin, *Resolving Social Conflicts* (New York: Harper, 1948), p. 74.
28. Deutsch, "Field Theory in Social Psychology," p. 199.
29. Ibid., p. 196.
30. Leon Festinger, Stanley Schachter, and Kurt Back, *Social Pressures in Informal Groups* (New York: Harper, 1950).
31. Deutsch, "Field Theory in Social Psychology," p. 215.
32. Kurt Back, "Influence through Social Communication," *Readings in Social Psychology*, rev. ed., ed. Guy E. Swanson, Theodore M. Newcomb, and Eugene L. Hartley (New York: Holt, 1952), pp. 445–459.
33. Cartwright and Zander, *Group Dynamics*, 3rd ed., pp. 99–103.
34. Stanley Schachter, Norris Ellertson, Dorothy McBride, and Doris Gregory, "An Experimental Study of Cohesiveness and Productivity," *Group Dynamics*, 3rd ed., pp. 192–198.
35. This summary follows Deutsch, "Field Theory in Social Psychology," p. 216.
36. Festinger, Schachter, and Back, *Pressures in Informal Groups*.
37. Leon Festinger and John Thibaut, "Interpersonal Communication in Small Groups," *Readings in Social Psychology*, rev. ed. (1952), p. 134.
38. Festinger, Schachter, and Back, *Pressures in Informal Groups*.
39. Harold Kelley, "Communication in Experimentally Created Hierarchies," *Group Dynamics*, 1st ed. (1953), p. 461.
40. John Thibaut, "An Experimental Study of the Cohesiveness of Underprivileged Groups," ibid., pp. 114–115. See also, Leon Festinger, "Informal Social Communication," ibid., chap. 15.
41. Deutsch, "Field Theory in Social Psychology," p. 218.
42. For a popular and enthusiastic account of the literature on democratic group leadership, see Donald A. and Eleanor C. Laird, *The*

New Psychology for Leadership (New York: McGraw-Hill, 1956). The Lairds say their report is "based on researches in Group Dynamics and Human Relations," but in the present author's opinion the Lairds are using the term "group dynamics" in its broad, non-capitalized, sense.

43. *Group Dynamics,* 1st ed. (1953), p. 88.
44. See Neal Gross and William E. Martin, "On Group Cohesiveness," *American Journal of Sociology* 57 (May 1957), the "Comment" by Stanley Schachter, and the "Rejoinder" by Gross and Martin. Another commentator has concluded that "as it now stands, cohesiveness is too general to explain anything in particular and so general as to describe anything one may wish it to designate." Robert S. Albert, "Comments on the Scientific Function of the Concept of Cohesiveness," ibid., 59 (November 1953), p. 233.
45. Robert F. Bales, *Interaction Process Analysis* (Chicago: University of Chicago Press, 1950), p. 61. © 1950 by The University of Chicago. Italics added. Bales' observations about groups apply to both men and women and to mixed groups, although the subjects used in his research were usually male undergraduates at Harvard University.
46. Ibid., pp. 15–16.
47. Ibid., p. 73.
48. Ibid., pp. 74–75.
49. Ibid., p. 76.
50. Ibid., p. 77.
51. Ibid., pp. 79–80.
52. See ibid., chap. 4. Also, Robert F. Bales, "Some Statistical Problems in Small Group Research," *Journal of the American Statistical Association* 46 (1951), pp. 311–322.
53. See George A. Talland, "Task and Interaction Process: Some Characteristics of Therapeutic Group Discussion," *Small Groups,* 1st ed. (1955), pp. 457–463.
54. See Robert F. Bales, "Some Uniformities of Behavior in Small Social Systems," *Readings in Social Psychology,* rev. ed. (1952), p. 152.
55. For discussion of these problems, see Michael S. Olmsted, "Small Group Interaction as a Function of Group Norms" (Ph.D. diss., Harvard University, 1952), chap. 6, sec. A. Also Talcott Parsons, Robert F. Bales, and Edward A. Shils, *Working Papers in the Theory of Action* (Glencoe, Ill.: Free Press, 1952), pp. 134ff.
56. Robert F. Bales, Fred L. Strodtbeck, Theodore M. Mills, and Mary E. Roseborough, "Channels of Communication in Small Groups," *American Sociological Review* 16 (August 1951).
57. Bales, "Some Uniformities of Behavior in Small Social Systems," p. 155.

58. Robert F. Bales and Fred L. Strodtbeck, "Phases in Group Problem-Solving," *Journal of Abnormal and Social Psychology* 46 (October 1951), p. 485.

59. Bales, *Interaction Process Analysis*, pp. 153–154.

60. Ibid., p. 156.

61. Ibid., p. 157.

62. Parsons, Bales, and Shils, *Working Papers in the Theory of Action*, p. 147.

63. Talcott Parsons and Robert F. Bales, *Family, Socialization and Interaction Process* (Glencoe, Ill.: Free Press, 1955), p. 290.

64. Ibid., p. 305. See also Talcott Parsons, "The Incest Taboo in Relation to Social Structure and the Socialization of the Child," *British Journal of Sociology* 5 (June 1954).

65. Robert F. Bales, *Personality and Interpersonal Behavior* (New York: Holt, Rinehart and Winston, 1970).

66. Albert Mehrabian, *Silent Messages* (Belmont, Calif.: Wadsworth, 1971). For additional references on nonverbal behavior, see A. Paul Hare, *Handbook of Small Group Research*, pp. 83–85.

chapter eight

1. Cf. Alvin W. Gouldner, *Studies in Leadership* (New York: Harper, 1950), Introduction. See also Cecil A. Gibb, "Leadership," *Handbook of Social Psychology*, 1st ed. vol. 2, pp. 877–920; Launor F. Carter, "Leadership and Small-Group Behavior," *Group Relations at the Crossroads*.

2. *Group Dynamics*, 3rd ed., p. 305.

3. Homans, *The Human Group*, p. 419.

4. Helen H. Jennings, "Leadership and Sociometric Choice," *Readings in Social Psychology*, rev. ed. (1952), p. 318.

5. Leonard Berkowitz, "Sharing Leadership in Small, Decision-Making Groups," *Small Groups*, 2nd ed., p. 678.

6. Donald G. Marquis, Harold Guetzkow, and Roger W. Heyns, "A Social Psychological Study of the Decision-Making Process."

7. Lauren G. Wispe, "Evaluating Section Teaching Methods in the Introductory Course," *Journal of Educational Research* 45 (November 1951). See also Philip Jacob, *Changing Values in College* (New York: Harper, 1958), chap. 5.

8. *Group Psychology and the Analysis of the Ego*, chaps. 6, 7.

9. See Émile Durkheim, *The Elementary Forms of the Religious Life* (Glencoe, Ill.: Free Press, 1947); and Kurt H. Wolff, *The Sociology of Georg Simmel* (Glencoe, Ill.: Free Press, 1950), pt. 3, chap. 4.

10. For a highly sophisticated theoretical treatment of legitimacy and group organization, see Max Weber, *The Theory of Social and Economic Organization*, sec. 1.

11. The relation of this paradigm to Bales' thinking seems to be roughly as follows: Of Bales' *observational categories*, 4 and 9 are relevant to cell 2; 6 and 7 to cell 1; 1, 2, 11, and 12 to cell 3; and 5 and 8 to cell 4. Categories 3 and 10 apply both to cell 2—"I agree" —and to cell 1—"I understand." Bales' earlier *theoretical role typology* relates to the present one as follows: access to resources = 2a; control over persons = 2b; status = 4a or 1b and 2b, depending on whether one emphasizes prestige or contribution to problem solution; solidarity = 3b. In Bales' later *empirical role typology*, his "idea man" may be equated with the paradigm roles 1a and 2a; his "guidance" man with 1b, 2b, and 3b; and his "best-liked" role with 3a. The "talking" role appears to be a measure of 2b and 1a. If these equations are reasonable, it is not surprising that Bales' "guidance" role is characterized as more generalized than the specialist "best-ideas" and "best-liked" roles, nor that the person in the "guidance" role is most often rated the group "leader." For some further revisionist reflections see Parsons and Bales, *Family, Socialization and Interaction Process*, p. 302.

12. The best evidence for the four dimensions is given in the thesis of Arthur S. Couch, "Psychological Determinants of Interpersonal Behavior" (Ph.D. diss., Harvard University, 1960).

13. Jerry S. Cloyd, "Patterns of Role Behavior in Informal Interaction," *Sociometry* 27, 2 (June 1964).

14. A summary of the AGIL Theory is given by Talcott Parsons in "An Outline of the Social System," ed. Talcott Parsons et al., *Theories of Society* (New York: Free Press, 1961), pp. 30–79, and also by Andrew Effrat, "Editor's Introduction" (Applications of Parsonian Theory), *Sociological Inquiry* 38 (Spring 1968).

15. A. Paul Hare, "Theories of Group Development and Categories for Interaction Analysis," *Small Group Behavior* 4, 3 (August 1973).

SELECTED READINGS

Bales, Robert F., *Interaction Process Analysis* (Cambridge: Addison-Wesley, 1950)
The basic statement of the author's point of view and procedure. A model of explicit argument relating microcosmic and macrocosmic dimensions.

Bales, Robert F., *Personality and Interpersonal Behavior* (New York: Holt, Rinehart and Winston, 1970)
A description of a method for classifying interpersonal behavior in terms of three dimensions. The method is designed to be used by a group member rather than a professional observer. Behavior ratings can be compared with descriptions of twenty-six personality types.

Berkowitz, Leonard, ed., *Advances in Experimental Social Psychology*, Vols. 1–4 (New York: Academic Press, 1964–1968)
A collection of reviews of various topics in experimental social psychology. Many of the reviews have relevance for the study of the small group.

Bion, W. R. *Experiences in Groups* (New York: Basic Books, 1961)
In a series of ruminative articles, an English psychiatrist reflects on the untoward character of humans in psychotherapeutic groups.

Cartwright, Dorwin, and Zander, Alvin, eds., *Group Dynamics: Research and Theory* (Evanston, Ill.: Row, Peterson, 1st ed., 1953; 3rd ed., 1968)
A collection of papers by various hands plus interpretive chapters by the editors, who are leading figures in the Group Dynamics school.

Freud, Sigmund, *Group Psychology and the Analysis of the Ego,* International Psychoanalytic Library (London: Hogarth Press, 1948)
A short but discursive explanation of group life in terms of the author's conception of the human personality.

Hare, A. Paul, *Handbook of Small Group Research,* 2nd ed. (New York: Free Press, 1976)
A summary of the major trends and findings in theory and research on small groups from 1898 through 1974. The bibliography includes over 6,000 references.

Hare, A. Paul, Borgatta, Edgar F., and Bales, Robert F., eds., *Small Groups: Studies in Social Interaction* (New York: Knopf, 1st ed., 1955; 2nd ed., 1965)
The first edition includes a collection of 55 excerpts and research reports representing many interests in the field of social psychology. It contains an annotated bibliography of 584 titles in the small-group field. The second edition contains more articles but no bibliography.

Homans, George C., *Social Behavior: Its Elementary Forms,* rev. ed. (New York: Harcourt, 1974)
A description of social behavior in small groups in terms of a theory of social exchange.

Homans, George C., *The Human Group* (New York: Harcourt, 1950)
A forthright and painstaking attempt to build a sociology on the basis of a comparative study of groups.

Laird, Donald A. and Eleanor C., *The New Psychology for Leadership* (New York: McGraw-Hill, 1956)
An enthusiastic account of how social scientists are getting people to work better together.

Lewin, Kurt, *Resolving Social Conflicts: Selected Papers on Group Dynamics* (New York: Harper & Row, 1948)
Reveals Lewin's practical and ameliorative concerns as well as his interest in experimentation in social science.

Lindzey, Gardner, ed., *Handbook of Social Psychology,* 2 vols. (Cambridge: Addison-Wesley, 1954)
An encyclopedic inventory. Contains chapters on Field Theory, on observational techniques, on sociometry, on leadership; and two overlapping surveys of small-group research.

Lindzey, Gardner, and Aronson, Elliot, eds., *Handbook of Social Psychology,* 5 vols., 2nd ed. (Reading, Mass.: Addison-Wesley, 1968)
A revision of the 1954 Lindzey volume that adds new material to supplement the original articles. Especially relevant is Volume 4 (1969) on "Group Psychology and the Phenomena of Interaction."

SELECTED READINGS

Moreno, J. L., ed., *The Sociometry Reader* (Glencoe, Ill.: Free Press, 1960)
A collection of articles covering the foundations, methods, major areas of exploration, and history of sociometry, the study of social structure as revealed in interpersonal choice.

Moreno, J. L., *Who Shall Survive?* rev. ed. (Beacon, N.Y.: Beacon House, 1953)
A detailed description of the various sociometric methods used by Moreno to change social institutions.

Shaw, Marvin E., *Group Dynamics: The Psychology of Small Group Behavior,* 2nd ed. (New York: McGraw-Hill, 1976)
A review of the literature on social behavior in small groups that combines the approaches of the Group Dynamics and "small groups" schools.

Shils, Edward A., "The Study of the Primary Group," in *The Policy Sciences,* ed. Daniel Lerner and Harold D. Lasswell, Hoover Institute Series (Stanford: Stanford University Press, 1951)
An even-tempered survey of points of view and contributions in the study of primary groups.

Swanson, Guy E., Newcomb, Theodore M., and Hartley, Eugene L., eds., *Readings in Social Psychology,* rev. ed. (New York: Holt, 1952). The third edition was edited by Eleanor E. Maccoby, Theodore M. Newcomb, and Eugene L. Hartley in 1958.
Contains a number of articles on small groups, constituting a handy introduction to some major tendencies in the field.

INDEX

Newcomb, Theodore M., study of interpersonal attraction, 31–35
Nietzsche, Friedrich, 143
1984 (Orwell), 52
Nisbet, Robert, on deracinated society, 49–50
nonverbal behavior, groups, 132–134
norms
  and culture, group, 88–92
  primary and secondary group, 92–93

observational categories, Bales' system of, 123
Olds, Bruce, 12n
Olmsted, Michael, 92
opinion research group, 36–38
organization
  group functions for, 43–44
  juvenile gang, 22
  see also leadership; social structure, group
Orwell, George, 52
output restriction, in Hawthorne studies, 18

Parsons, Talcott, 4, 145
particularism vs. universalism, 46–47
pattern maintenance, 145–146
perception of individual, group's effect on, 66–68
permissive leadership, as "segregated," 143
personality, group effect on, 80–81
personal primary group, 50–51
  and tyranny, 50, 52–53
phase movement, groups, 126
Piaget, Jean, 40
potency and nonverbal behavior, 132

pressures to conform
  interpretation of, 68–73
  yielding to, 67–68
primary group
  common code, 19–20
  Cooley's concept of, 7–8
  dysfunctions for individual, 42–43
  functions for individual, 39–42
  functions for organization, 43–44
  functions for society, 44–55
  norms, vs. secondary group, 92–93
  vs. small group, 12–13
  society as, 55–57
  see also group(s); group behavior; social structure, group
primordial primary group, 50, 52
problem-solving, group, 85–88
process and culture, group, 82–85
profiles, groups, 125
propinquity and personal primary group, 50–51
psychegroup vs. sociogroup, 96–97
psychoanalysis, 96–101
psychodrama, 74, 96
psychotherapy, group, 73–74

The Quest for Community (Nisbet), 49

rank differentiation, group, 108
Redfield, Robert, 9
Redl, Fritz, 142
  concept of group leadership, 99–100
relational analysis, 96
resources, access to, 120

ABOUT THE AUTHORS

Michael Seymour Olmsted, late assistant professor of sociology and anthropology at Smith College, was graduated cum laude from Harvard University and received the M.Ed. at the Graduate Teachers College of Winnetka, the M.A. at the University of Chicago, and the Ph.D. at Harvard University. At Harvard he held teaching fellowships in social relations and general education, and in 1952 he became an instructor in the Department of Sociology at Smith College, where he taught until his death in 1960. He served as editor of the *American Sociological Review*, in which he published "Orientation and Role in the Small Group." He also published articles and reviews in the *American Journal of Sociology*, *Social Forces*, and the *Smith College Quarterly*.

A. Paul Hare is Chairman of the Department of Sociology at the University of Capetown in Rondebosch, South Africa, where he has taught since 1973. He received the Ph.D. at the University of Chicago, after which he served as a research and teaching assistant at Harvard University. He taught at Haverford College from 1960 to 1973. Editor of *Sociological Inquiry* from 1967 to 1970, Professor Hare has published extensively in that journal as well as in other leading sociology publications including *Sociometry, Journal of Social Psychology,* and *Small Group Behavior.* With E. F. Borgatta and R. F. Bales he edited *Small Groups: Studies in Social Interaction,* and with H. H. Blumberg he edited *Nonviolent Direct Action* and *Liberation without Violence.* He is the author of the *Handbook of Small Group Research.* Currently, he specializes in the areas of small group research, computer simulation of interpersonal behavior, and nonviolent direct action.